8 Habits of an Effective Youth Worker

8 Habits
of an Effective
Youth Worker

Tim Smith

VICTOR BOOKS

A DIVISION OF SCRIPTURE PRESS PUBLICATIONS INC.
USA CANADA ENGLAND

Cover design by Joe DeLeon
Cartoon illustrations by Lindy

Library of Congress Cataloging-in-Publication Data

Smith, Tim, 1954—
    Eight habits of an effective youth worker / Tim Smith.
      p.   cm.
    Includes bibliographical references.
    ISBN 1-56476-406-0
    1. Church work with teenagers. I. Title.
  BV4447.S634   1995
  259′.23—dc20   94-42553
                                                  CIP

2 3 4 5 6 7 8 9 10 Printing/Year 99 98 97 96 95

Produced for Victor Books by the Livingstone Corporation. David Veerman, Michael Kendrick, and Brenda James Todd, project staff.

What People Are Saying about
Eight Habits of an Effective Youth Worker
by Tim Smith

Eight Habits of an Effective Youth Worker is one of the first books to be written from a new paradigm of youth work. It's very much a holistic approach to reaching and ministering to kids. The focus on the inner life of the youth worker is wonderful. All of us in youth work need this book.

Jim Burns
President
National Institute of Youth Ministry

Eight Habits of an Effective Youth Worker by Tim Smith is a blueprint for developing character in the life of the youth worker. It offers a fresh, practical, and biblical strategy to develop leaders with integrity and impact. Tim reminds us that effective youth ministry is not simply creativity and skill, but an issue of the heart. If you have a passion for youth and a zeal for effectiveness, read *Eight Habits*.

Dr. Barry St. Clair
Reach Out Ministries

In a world where many youth workers get caught in the performance trap of bigger and better, Tim Smith, in his book, *Eight Habits of an Effective Youth Worker*, calls youth work back to its basics—back to the things which will really make youth ministry effective, and that is the heart, the mind, and the spirit of the youth worker. This is not a book of how-to's. It is a book of character and integrity and a book that calls us to be people of God. This book is must reading for any youth worker serving kids today.

Dr. Daniel Hahn
Pastor of Students and Families,
Mission Hills Church
Adjunct Professor of Youth Ministry,
Talbot School of Theology and Biola University

Eight Habits of an Effective Youth Worker is must reading for anyone desiring to be involved in youth ministry for the long haul. The "habits" Tim encourages youth workers to develop are not meant to be tricks of the trade, but building blocks of character, passion, and effectiveness that will lay a firm foundation for solid ministry.

Jim Marian
High School Pastor
Lake Avenue Congregational Church
Pasadena, CA

Dedicated to three mentors
who have shaped my life:

Jack Monroe—who modeled for me effective
youth work in my early years.

Rick Yohn—who encouraged me to dream big
and take risks—like writing.

Larry DeWitt—who reminds me that the core of the
Gospel is from the heart.

Contents

FOREWORD

I had just walked off the stage at what the sponsors referred to as one of the largest youth events ever held in their state. The music had been wonderful. The spirit of excitement in the crowd was electric. I believe I felt God's spirit in my message and the response to a call to commitment was absolutely overwhelming. What a night!

A woman I had known for several years from a distance came right up to me afterward. Her husband had been a spiritual mentor in my life and he had recently left his position of leadership because of sexual immorality. She gave me a hug and with tears in her eyes said, "Jim, untended fires soon become nothing but a pile of ashes." Her words threw me. I had expected, "Isn't God wonderful?" or "Good job." But instead I got, "Untended fires soon become nothing but a pile of ashes." My special friend had experienced the same youth event as me. She had seen the excitement of the kids. She watched the intense response of the students as they made beautiful commitments to our Lord Jesus Christ. But, frankly, she had been there before. She and her husband's life work had been to serve Jesus and, for most of their years, they had had phenomenal fruit in the area of youth ministry. She also knew firsthand the depth of pain of a broken relationship, and of sin and failure in the ministry. In a sense she had experienced "the thrill of victory and the agony of defeat."

Now she was approaching me with what I believe was a message from God: "untended fires soon become nothing but a pile of ashes." As I read this wonderful book of Tim Smith's, I can't help but think back to days of very few youth ministry resources and only a handful of "professional" youth workers. They were days with no youth ministry magazines, few conferences, little training, and a lot of prayer. Those who chose youth work were the weird ones. (Perhaps they still are today!) I look at those times as a season of burning desire to reach students with the Gospel of Jesus Christ. We would do anything to get their attention. I remember swallowing goldfish and shaving my beard just to get students out to an event! Needless to say, the programs have changed, we have quality resources, and the training is outstanding.

It's a new generation of youth work with new problems and changing issues. *Eight Habits of an Effective Youth Worker* is one of the first books to be written from a new paradigm of youth work. It's very much a holistic approach to reaching and ministering to kids. The focus on the inner life of the youth worker is wonderful. Tim is helping youth workers see that untended fires soon become nothing but a pile of ashes.

In case you haven't had the privilege to meet Tim Smith, he is an exceptional youth worker who has "made the turn" to a newer paradigm shift in youth work. He knows what he is talking about and is doing youth work today in a fresh new format. Tim's approach to family ministry, culture, team ministry, and administration is refreshingly new material.

It was a joy to read this book and I know you'll be a more effective youth worker for having walked down the path Tim takes you on. All of us in youth work need this book. Youth ministry is one of the most exciting and influential areas of the church and we must establish some healthy habits in order to face the daily battle for the lives of our kids. Thank you for your commitment to student ministry, and thank God for people like yourselves who are influencing more students for eternity than you will ever imagine.

Jim Burns
President
National Institute of Youth Ministry

The Passion for Quality

What lies behind us and what lies before us are tiny matters compared to what lies within us.[1]

Within the soul of every youth worker there is a passion for kids. A passion to impact them in the most significant and lasting way. It's more than liking to "work with kids," it's an intense desire for influence. If it was just a matter of hanging around adolescents, we could be managers at the video arcade in the mall. But what drives us who minister to youth is the hope that we might be able to benefit the teens and impact the world for the Kingdom of Christ.

It is this passion for quality which will bring about a renaissance in youth ministry in the final decade of the millennium. We are living in an era of cataclysmic change, old walls are knocked down, new ones are erected. Some people are liberated, while others are held hostage by poverty, violence, famine, and religious fanaticism.

It is within this environment that we seek to minister. In the '60s we witnessed the explosion of the *Rally* and *Big Event* youth ministry. In the '70s we experienced the Jesus movement and the growth of worship and small group Bible study. In the '80s we observed much emphasis on church growth, *Bigger is Better* (quantity) mentality in youth work. In the '90s we are enjoying a growing passion for **quality**. The economics of the day and the crisis within the culture demand that we produce quality.

A Culture in Crisis

More and more children across the nation are being born into families with a great likelihood of falling into poverty, mainly because so many teenagers are having babies.[2]

Those of us who minister to teens know how devastating a teenage pregnancy can be. These risks increase the chances that families will break up, be poor, or be dependent on public assistance and that their children will be neglected and fall behind in school.[3]

Effective youth ministry is essential if we are going to break the downward spiral of immobility caused by the fallout of these adolescent problems. But how are kids supposed to make good decisions? Their own parents have let them down, and let each other down.

The disappearance of marriage as a dependable, permanent structure within which children can live out their childhood is surely the most consequential change that has occurred in the last two decades.[4]

Divorce is usually traumatic for teens. The breakup of their family confuses roles. The teen may have to act like a parent and assume responsibility because the parent is acting like a child. These issues of rejection, desertion, separation, and loss have an incredible impact on the parent as well as the teen. In time, the parent may recover, but the adolescent will never be the same—their innocence will never be recaptured. They experienced the wages and burden of divorce and may be frightened by what they saw. Children of divorce discover that their parents are often as helpless, confused, and vulnerable as they themselves are. In the quiet, dark hours they may lie awake and worry, "Who will take care of me if my parents can't even take care of themselves?"

As a result of family breakup, a teen becomes more vulnerable to the stresses of modern life.

Statistically, children of divorce are more likely to become involved with alcohol and drugs, to commit suicide, to get in trouble with the law, to fail in school. And as time goes on, new and troubling connections are being uncovered between the children of divorce and a host of grave social problems, from runaways to sexual abuse and even mass hysteria.[5]

To be effective in youth ministry we need to look at teens in their environment. "What kind of environment does she live in?" "What kind of emotional climate does he go home to?" Gone are the days when we could deal with the teen as an individual with no regard to their environment. We need to do EIR's (Environmental Impact Reports) on our teens to discover the systems they live in.

An environmental approach to youth ministry will prepare us to face the crisis in our culture. It will help us by creating windows into the souls of our kids. Then we will genuinely understand what lies within them.

A Commitment to Character

We don't have the luxury to play around with youth ministry anymore; we need to work at it. A cosmetic approach which deals with externals like numbers, dollars, and celebrities won't cut it in a world of chaos and change. These become "tiny matters" when we look at the core issues—the matters of the heart. In a culture that is drowning with a deluge of voices and information, it is character that communicates most effectively. As Ralph Waldo Emerson said, "What you are shouts so loudly in my ears I cannot hear what you say." What we *are* communicates more eloquently than anything we *say* or *do*.

We used to be able to focus on the youth as an individual, entertain him a little and then slip in a little something about God—that was youth ministry. It's all changed—the stakes are much higher; teens are more fragile, more susceptible to stress, and now face an array of at-risk behavior choices. We need to build into them a commitment to growth in character—growth from the inside out. The best way to begin this is to model it ourselves.

The character ethic is based on the fundamental idea that there are *principles* that govern human effectiveness—natural laws in the human dimension that are just as real, just as unchanging and arguably "there" as laws such as gravity are in the physical dimension.[6]

There are principles for effective youth ministry. These are to be contrasted with practices which are culturally, demographically or situationally specific. In other words, practices may work in Boise, but they may fail in Boston. Principles differ from practices because they are proven, fundamental truths that have universal application. Principles are transferable from situation to situation. If a principle is true, it will be effective in Boise *and* Boston. When principles are integrated into a person's thinking, they begin to shape his character. In time, this character-shaping results in a habit based on principles. Effective habits are behaviors that are desirable and based on principles. Our goal then, is to study the habits of effective youth workers and personally integrate timeless truths into our thinking. If we have principles, we will have lasting, permanent guidelines that will serve as a compass in our journey towards effective youth ministry.

AN INTRODUCTION TO THE 8 HABITS OF AN EFFECTIVE YOUTH WORKER

These habits will be fully developed later in the book, but I wanted to introduce you to all eight now so they can be cooking on your back burner.

#1 Effective Youth Workers *Are Committed to Lifelong Learning*

Approaching life as a learner, rather than a teacher creates the perspective for growth. If we are learners, we interpret all of life's situations and experiences as opportunities for learning and personal involvement.

A few years ago Peter, my fellow coworker in youth ministry, and I went to a national youth convention in San Francisco. We met a youth pastor from Texas in the lobby who was looking for a tour of San Francisco. He had the rented car, and we knew San Francisco (well, kind of—at least better than he!). As he pulled out of the hotel parking lot he asked,

"How big is your church?"

"About 1,500 on Sundays," Peter replied.

"Do you have a large youth group?" inquired Tex.

"No, not really, we only have about twenty committed kids," I explained.

This was a strategy Peter and I had decided on because we were getting tired of "group envy" which often is rampant at youth worker's conventions. We decided a canned response like this would focus on the heart of youth ministry, not the height or weight of our group. We agreed to always say, "twenty committed kids" and see what the response would be. Tex fell right into it.

"Well, in Blue Rock we have a membership of 4,000, youth membership of around 1,000, a bus ministry, twenty-two buses, a full-time bus mechanic, a Christian school, a gymnasium that we call "Family Center," and a new sanctuary that will seat 1,000," bragged Tex as he drove down Market Street soaking in the exotic smells and sights of the city.

Tex continued his tall tale of pastoral bravado all the way through our authentic Chinese meal in authentic China Town. When he excused himself to use the "little cowboy's room," Peter and I toyed with the idea of ditching him in China Town, but we were at a "Christian" convention. It might be hard to face him later on, especially if Tony Compolo was preaching on compassion and ethics!

Tex reminds me that learners are listeners. He didn't listen to us the whole evening. If he asked a question, he only used it to introduce what he was doing, which was infinitely superior (at least by his account). Peter and I were struggling with our youth group. At the time, we really could have used a good listener, or even a creative problem solver. Instead, we got trapped in a cheap rental car with a person who got his mouth stuck in the gear of self-promotion. It was a sad evening. Instead of being an opportunity to exchange ideas, support, and encourage each other and learn, it was a night of empty rhetoric, disrespect, and on top of it all, bad sweet and sour pork!

A year later at the convention someone was talking about the "scandal at Blue Rock." "What happened there?" I inquired.

"Tex was fired; he had an affair with one of the girls in his high school group. His wife is divorcing him too."

I wasn't surprised; my impression was that Tex was a talker, not a learner. He obviously needed to learn at that San Francisco convention. Sometimes I wonder if that year he was struggling too.

#2 Effective Youth Workers *Are Service Oriented*

We lead best when we seek the welfare of those we lead; when we seek to serve rather than being served. This was the secret to Christ's impact; "The greatest among you will be your servant" (Matthew 23:11).

An effective youth worker never forgets that she is in a service career. We are here to understand the needs of the customer and be responsive to those needs. Like a good waiter or a caring shepherd, an effective youth worker anticipates needs and seizes the opportunity to minister to those in need. Sometimes we forget the metaphor of servant-leadership and buy into the corporate mentality of leadership which is based on position and power. We become obsessed with leading a large group and ministering to the masses. It is at these times that we need to learn from the Master who, even though He spoke to thousands, He took time to:

Bless a young boy who shared his lunch.

Heal a bleeding woman.

Bring to life a little girl.

Talk to a short man in a tree.

Heal a blind man.

These people weren't the politically correct people of His culture, they were the average people—the "nobodies"; they weren't the "movers and shakers" of Palestine.

Jesus was able to be service-oriented because he understood his mission. He was able to focus on the individual because he respected each person. That is what the parable of the lost sheep is all about. Effective youth workers don't forget about the lost sheep, even though they may have ninety-nine in the fold. Maybe that is what Dag Hammarskjold, past Secretary General of the United Nations, had in mind when he said, "It is more noble to give yourself completely to one individual than to labor diligently for the salvation of the masses."

People who lead lives of impact know the value of personal service and commitment to the individual.

#3 Effective Youth Workers *Radiate the Positive Power of the Holy Spirit*

Much of what we read about in management books is about "being positive" or the right use of power. I've often read these and thought, "Sometimes I just don't feel like being positive, and I want to grab as much power as I can!" Being a continually positive leader who never abuses his position is not only difficult—it's impossible! Using the tools of our culture to minister effectively is destined to failure. To minister effectively, we need complete dependence on the Holy Spirit. Our natural gifts and abilities will synergize with our spiritual gifts to provide us with the tools we need to impact youth for Christ's kingdom.

The good news with this habit is that it does not depend on our strengths to be effective. In fact, when I am tired or perplexed, I often have the most significant times of ministry.

> My grace is sufficient for you, for my power is made perfect in weakness. Therefore I will boast all the more gladly about my weaknesses, so that Christ's power may rest on me. That is why for Christ's sake, I delight in weaknesses, in insults, in hardships, in persecutions, in difficulties. For when I am weak, then I am strong (2 Corinthians 12:9-10).

Christ's power can be made perfect in my weakness. In fact, I can boast of my weaknesses to create more of a vacuum for Christ's power! Now, that's a deal!

#4 Effective Youth Workers *Believe in Others (and Their Growth)*

I have been working with my staff to help them "expect the best from the people you lead." It recently got me in trouble. We were planning a large event and had recruited several capable volunteers to assist five of our paid staff in developing this big event. I had a few meetings with my paid staff and we developed an overall strategy for the event and assigned them to develop the specifics. They discussed the event with their volunteers and decided to make changes and improvements on the event. I had given them the freedom to do this because I trusted them and they are the ones who know the ministry best. One of the church elders was upset because, "It doesn't sound like what we thought it was going to be. Tell them to change it! Why didn't you check on them and keep this from getting out of hand?" he challenged. "Because I trust them to develop the best possible event for the kids—they are experts, and I have confidence in them. This plan is better, we'll stick with it " I responded. It was risky, but it paid off. Minutes later, one of the leaders confided in private, "I've observed that you operate from a position of trust, Elder Ernie operates from a position of distrust. Now I know why people like to work with you." I was delighted to see that my recent efforts to offer others my confidence and to build on their strengths and minimize their weaknesses was actually paying off.

#5 Effective Youth Workers *Lead Balanced Lives*

In rock climbing, surfing, and youth ministry, balance is crucial. It seems to me that most problems we encounter in youth ministry come from the extremes. Mature and effective youth workers have learned to balance competing demands. Fundamental to balance is the ability to say "no." If we are always saying "yes" to every opportunity, our time will be eroded by the pressing urgencies we have created. I have a rule of thumb, "Try to say 'no' to something everyday." It's liberating and quite fun once you get into it. Just today another pastor on staff asked me if I'd help with the Day of Prayer. He had a few reasons why he thought I should help plan it. I said "No, thanks, I'm already doing some other extra projects." It felt great! He responded, "Okay, I'll ask Gordy if he'd like to help." No pain, no guilt.

Youth workers with balance have committed themselves to make skillful use of their time and their time-focus. They are able to balance their focus between the past, the present, and the future. They are willing to learn from the past and control their present schedules in order to impact their future. Balance also has to do with an awareness of one's strengths and weaknesses. Balanced leaders aren't perfect, but they've discovered a way to capitalize on their strengths and compensate for their weaknesses.

Have you noticed that people you like to spend time with are able to laugh at themselves? A sense of humor is a trait of a balanced life. Humor is common in youth workers, but many times it is cynical, sarcastic, or demeaning. It's humor with a sting. Laughing at ourselves is healthier and less risky. I'm not advocating putting ourselves down, just use your own life as a source of humor—if you do, you'll never run out of material!

#6 Effective Youth Workers *See Life as an Adventure*

Not only are effective youth workers lifelong learners, but they are on a safari to jungles unknown. They are risk-takers who know that life is a mission that demands taking expeditions into new and unchartered territories. If comfort, stability, and security are your aspirations, then get out of youth ministry. Flexibility, change, and risk are what you are more likely to encounter in the youth ministry jungle. True security comes from within, not from without.

We don't need to categorize or stereotype life to give us a degree of certainty and predictability. Anyone who truly knows adolescents knows that *predictability* is antithetical to teens.

If we see life as an adventure, then we have the paradigm to experience what Christ was discussing in John 10:10, "I have come that they may have life and have it to the full." Adventure-minded leaders are eager to learn from every teen they encounter. They don't categorize them according to externals or their past. They see within each teen the potential for them to lead life to the fullest in Christ and to join the adventure of pursuing His kingdom.

#7 Effective Youth Workers *Are Team Players and Synergistic*

Synergy is the state in which the whole is more than the sum of the parts. Synergistic youth ministry affirms the value and contribution of each individual. A youth worker who understands synergy will be able to make students and staff feel valuable by affirming their individual contribution and uniqueness. She will also be able to show individuals how their contribution and giftedness benefits the whole group. As each person feels valued, affirmed, and meaningful, a spirit of teamwork begins to develop. This "esprit de corps" is a result of relationship, relevance, and rallying people together. Synergy can't be forced, contrived, or manufactured—it must be grown. As it grows, it begins to take on a life of its own. This life is energy produced by the cooperative spirit of people effectively working together.

Synergy is a modern word for a concept that is 2,000 years old.

> If you have any encouragement from being united with Christ, if any comfort from His love, if any fellowship with the Spirit, if any tenderness and compassion, then make my joy complete by being like-minded, having the same love, being one in spirit and purpose. Do nothing out of selfish ambition or vain conceit, but in humility consider others better than yourselves. Each of you should look not only to your own interests, but also to the interests of others (Philippians 2:1-4).

Effective youth workers with an understanding of synergy find it easier to recruit volunteers because people are seeking the encouragement, the love, and focused fellowship that comes as a result of spiritual teamwork.

#8 Effective Youth Workers *Are Committed to Personal Renewal*

Anyone who has been in youth work knows that ministry is a drain of energy and passion. To be continually effective, youth workers need a strategy for personal renewal. We need to know what it is in our work that drains us. We need to recognize our symptoms of fatigue, and have a standard to evaluate just how worn out we really are.

Youth work is more passion than profession. If we are drained physically, emotionally, or spiritually, all the degrees on the wall won't help us shepherd our kids. It is crucial that a youth worker have those times and places of renewal. Maybe we are most like Christ when we are in that lonely place seeking renewal.

> At daybreak Jesus went out to a solitary place. The people were looking for Him and when they came to where He was, they tried to keep Him from leaving them (Luke 4:42).

There will always be needs and people pressing on us for our attention, but it is imperative that we seek to refresh our souls so we minister out of fullness, not out of emptiness. One of the saddest sights I've seen are the hollow, blank eyes of a burnt-out youth worker who has lost his passion due to a lack of personal renewal.

The privilege of ministry is growth. To be effective we need to make sure we are modeling to our students and leaders a person who is growing because he is being renewed—physically, emotionally, and spiritually.

Discussion Questions

1. Do you agree that effective youth work requires a passion for kids—an intense desire for influence?

2. What disturbs you most about our culture?

3. Why is it so easy to get caught up in the "numbers game"?

4. How does an effective youth worker balance his/her/their focus between the past, the present, and the future?

5. Synergy is the state in which the whole is more than the sum of the parts. Describe a time when you observed synergy.

6. Do you agree or disagree with the statement, "Youth work is more passion than profession"?

NOTES

1. Oliver Wendell Holmes.

2. Center for the Study of Social Policy AP—Washington, March 29, 1993.

3. Judith Weitz, Coordinator of Research for *Kids Count Data Book,* Associated Press—wire, March 29, 1993.

4. Marie Winn, *Children without Childhood* (New York: Pantheon Books, 1993), 125.

5. Ibid., 134.

6. Stephen Covey, *The 7 Habits of Highly Effective People: Powerful Lessons in Personal Change (New York: Simon & Schuster, Inc., 1989), 32.*

CHAPTER TWO

Bend with the Trends

Habit #1—"Effective Youth Workers Are
Lifelong Learners"

I t was the era of long hair, Birkenstock sandals, and tie-dye T-shirts—the '60s. Being a youth worker meant you were teaching kids "Radical Discipleship." It meant backpacking with the youth group and having heavy rap sessions (the kind you talk at, not dance to). It was the time for individuals to pursue their own journey. People had their own thing to get into. The youth in the church didn't trust the establishment old-folks. The old folks hoped the youth director they hired would "teach these kids to respect their elders." In some regions, there was a real strong nationalism, "USA—Love It or Leave It." Others struggled with a war that made little sense, and a growing mistrust in government and leadership in general.

In the '70s we had learned to "hang loose" and "let it be." It was a time of mixed messages. On one hand, we tried to be cool; on the other hand we were really mad. The key word within the church became "renewal." The focus became revolutionizing structures that were old and ineffective.

MOD SQUAD

Those days, I had my hair in a big puffy afro, wore shorts and sandals, and carried a book in my backpack *The Problem of Wineskins: Church Structure in a Technological Age* by Howard Snyder. It called for radical change. The church must be structured so as to affirm the uniqueness and value of human personality. It must insist that what is true of individual human persons is equally true of the church: It has value because it is a work of God.[1]

Snyder called for a new look at the church and the affirmation of the value of the individual. The individual human was at risk in the '70s, technology was crouching at the door waiting to clone us all into the "Stepford Wives." Snyder warned, "The church today lives in a world increasingly hostile to all that is human."[2]

If you worked with youth in the '70s, maybe you remember the Sunday School lessons you taught, fellowship on Sunday nights, the Wednesday night youth groups, the "Fifth Quarters" after the football games, or how about those "Lock-Ins"? You enjoyed seeing the kids in the youth group three or four times a week. When you had sign-ups for camps, you always had to make a waiting list.

Times have changed, haven't they? Those of you who weren't involved in youth ministry in the '70s probably can't relate to this seemingly fictional narrative. There has been so much change, it's almost impossible to relate to the '70s. Yet, many of us still minister like we did then. How about you? Do you still minister the way you did in the '70s? In the '80s?

Consider all the "right here, right now, waking up to history" going around us: the Wall came down, the Eastern Bloc disenfranchised itself from the Soviet Union, which itself fell apart. Missionaries are being sent to Eastern Europe from Africa and Latin America. The world is in flux.

If we are to be effective and relevant youth workers, we need to learn to think trends, not tradition. We also need to evaluate our existing ministries to see if they reflect an awareness of the changes of our world. A '70s wineskin won't cut it in the '90s.

Consider the contrasts:

THE WAY IT WAS—'70s	**THE WAY IT'S GOING—'90s**
Long hair	Shaved head
Tie-dye T-Shirt	Dockers pants
TV Family—"Brady Bunch"	"Frasier"
3 TV Networks	100 Cable choices
Slogan—"Hang Loose"	"Just Do It!"
Verbal	Visual
Office	Home office
Personal freedom	Control over environment
Desire for information	Desire for simplicity
FM radio	MTV and CD's

THE WAY IT WAS—'70s	THE WAY IT'S GOING—'90s
Loyalty/commitment	Options/choices
Most important resource—money	Most important resource—time
Full service	Nichemanship
Data-driven	Need-driven
Change seen as optional	Change seen as mandatory
Individual	Group/family systems
Self-help	Network
Denial regarding dysfunction	Dysfunction is common
Most boomers reject the church	Many boomers return to church
Intellectual solutions	Emotional resolutions
Decline in religion	Increase in spirituality
Outer structure reform	Inner recovery
Values—issues and altruism	Values—tangible benefit
Reform existing structure	Entrepreneurial—new
Top-down	Bottom-up
Outside-in	Inside-out
Pastor-centered leadership	Team-centered leadership
Male dominated leadership	Women and men in leadership
Church as program	Church as relationships
Teaching center	Resource center
Casual, hang loose	Excellence, professional
Guru: John Lennon	Guru: Rush Limbaugh
Taboo: Stale thinking	Taboo: Political incorrectness
What's in: Experimentation	What's in: Recovery

Learning from the Contrasts

Understanding the changes from decade to decade will help the perceptive youth worker to know how to effectively minister. Ministry is finding a need and meeting it. If we are aware of trends within our culture, we will be able to be relevant to the youth we serve. To be relevant, we need to be current. It has been my experience that the church tends to change and adopt to the needs of society five to ten years after the shift. If we are to be relevant, we need to be current with cultural shifts and trends.

Relevancy has a qualitative aspect to it as well. We need to be offering a youth ministry of substance and excellence. George Barna discusses effective churches:

> Undeniably, working with kids these days is a fascinating experience. The leaders at the growing churches concurred that ministering to children and youth today is even more demanding than in the past. Raised in a society in which cut throat competition is commonplace, they are exposed to excellence in the quality

of products and services, and they have come to expect excellence from the church too. Today's young people are quality driven. They are not willing to accept mediocrity or to put up with ministry that is in a maintenance mode.[3]

We used to be able to get by with strumming a few chords on the guitar and singing "Pass It On." Now, kids expect a praise band, complete with synthesizer, electronic drums, worship leaders with choreography, and lyrics projected on a 8' x 10' screen. At youth groups in the '70s we were casual, kicked-back, and weren't concerned with excellence. In fact, sloppiness was in. In 1975 I taught a six month series on Acts in a black-widow spider infested "youth shack," and the kids packed it out!

Kids are much more sophisticated in the '90s. They aren't necessarily more mature, just more selective—they are used to having many options. A youth ministry that says "Here we are! This is what we offer—fit into our programs" is destined to fail. If we are to be lifelong learners, we need to be students of our own kids in the youth group. Ministry must be sensitive to three things to be effective in the '90s:

(1) Be sensitive to your students' different *levels of maturity*. Not all students are interested in what you may be offering. Your "Fellowship" program may be perceived as "for only those without a social life." Your Bible study could be too challenging for some and boring to others. We need to assess the various levels of maturity and interest of our students and ask ourselves, "What do we have that meets them at this level and challenges them towards the next level of maturity?"

(2) Be sensitive to your students' *time restrictions*. It used to be possible to see your students come to a youth event three or four times in one week. Now, time is our students' most important resource. We need to assess our expectations regarding students' time.

Dan Smith, our high school pastor, and I recently went through an evaluation period of our high school ministry. Realizing that we weren't making the kind of impact we wanted to make in our community, we began asking ourselves questions.

- What are our attendance patterns?
- What kind of student is coming to each ministry?
- How are we ministering to different levels of maturity/interest?
- How have we demonstrated a sensitivity to the students' time restrictions?

As we considered these questions with our student leaders and adult staff, a few discoveries became very illuminating. We discovered that we had two weekly programs that had become quite blurred in their purpose. Our Tuesday night outreach, "Campus Connection" was moderately successful in connecting with pre-Christian students. We found it difficult to recruit staff for this program even though it was a high energy night with innovative recreation, multi-media, music, drama, and short "safe" talks on hot topics. Our Sunday evening "Power Surge" was designed to be a growth-level event that challenged Christian students to apply Biblical principles to their lives. We had a different staff team for each night, and students generally drifted towards one or the other. Even though our program looked good on paper, it wasn't having the impact we wanted. What had happened? Was the program weak? Why had we lost the attendance and the spiritual growth we had seen earlier?

I believe the program had not become weaker, but out of step with the students. Losing sight of the cultural trends had caused us to be unrealistic in our expectations. We had expected students to come on their own to Saturday or Sunday Celebrations (our corporate worship times), attend Sunday night for Bible study and then invite their friends to a campus-oriented outreach Tuesday night. On top of this, we were offering monthly weekend events and camps. For our culture, this was too much. It created subtle pressure on the students to be involved at a level that most weren't able to maintain. It created an unnecessary gulf between the adult ministry teams from each program. We were feeling guilty because we weren't able to generate enough energy to draw students for a weekly outreach event. It had also made some student leaders feel they were "being used." One sixteen-year-old leader said "You use us to get our friends here and to help with the little things, but you really don't trust us with the big decisions of our group." This comment jarred us into remembering that in the '90s students want:

- to be involved
- to have choices
- to work on a team
- to have their needs met (not simply run a program)
- excellence

(3) Be sensitive to your students' desire for *something meaningful*. For youth ministry to be effective in the '90s, we need a renewed commitment to have activities that are inherently meaningful and make them fun. For decades, we have had fun events and struggled to infuse meaning into them. Many times I've felt like Jon Lovett's Pathological Liar when after an hour of crowd breakers and games, I segue with, "The point of the pie toss and pig wrestling was to show us . . . the messiness of sin. Yeah, that's it!" Sometimes we really stretch to reach meaningfulness. Students are looking for things to do which are meaningful *and* fun. If we start out with fun always being the

top priority we usually end up running out of resources (time, money, ideas, people, or energy) before we make it meaningful.

Effective ministry now means being the right person more than developing the right program. Students are bored with programs, they are too busy for hype. They want events to be fun, certainly, but they must also be meaningful.

Seasons of a Ministry

To be relevant to our students, we needed to make changes in our ministry. We started with these three ideas in mind:

1. Be sensitive to your students' differing levels of maturity.
2. Be sensitive to your students' time restrictions.
3. Be sensitive to your students' desire for something meaningful.

Ministries go through seasons. What works in the "fall" of a ministry may die in the "winter". The wise youth worker is sensitive to the seasons of a ministry and is courageous enough to make the necessary adjustments.

In our ministry it meant being willing to do less, in order to do a better job at what we did. "Nichemanship" is the idea of focusing in on what you do well and pouring your resources into that. It has a lot to do with giftedness. Having a full-service youth ministry with multiple programs, large budgets and several staff teams is unrealistic for most of us. Simplicity and excellence will become marks of effective youth ministries. Keeping this in mind, we've gone to a simpler, gentler, kinder youth program. We now ask our adult leaders and kids to come out one night a week, and to make that a priority. Instead of Sunday night Bible study we meet Tuesday nights for "Power Surge" which begins with a time of worship, followed by a short, creative Bible lesson and then break up into small groups for forty-five minutes. The continuity of always meeting in the same group with the same leader has facilitated interpersonal relationships amongst students and with their leader. Groups are encouraged to plan activities outside group time around a common interest. This has proven to be effective because it is flexible, personal, meaningful, and relational.

Every seven weeks we attempt an effective outreach. We encourage the Christian students in their small groups to identify and pray for friends that they are going to invite to the outreach ("Campus Connection").

Our staff now has the freedom to develop media, music, drama, and program for an event that accomplishes our goal of making contact with pre-Christians.

Learning to Risk Change

Making major program changes used to be considered risky in youth ministry. We used to look at change as optional, but considering the trends we face in our culture, change is mandatory. The real risk involved is thinking traditionally and not staying relevant to the needs of our youth. Like the leaves that drop from the trees in the fall, some elements of your ministry may need to be dropped from season to season. As the gardener prunes a branch in early spring so it will bear more blossoms later in the season, you too may need to prune a branch off your youth ministry to produce more fruitfulness. Successful ministry in this era certainly isn't bigger and better, it's simplicity and effectiveness. Instead of building a Rolls Royce with all the amenities, we need to build a Jeep that is simple, rugged, durable, and flexible. Your most effective ministry planning tool may be your eraser.

Church growth can be described as taking off of the Body of Christ all outmoded or ineffective garments, and clothing it instead with garments that identify it as the attractive Bride of Christ.

> Growing congregations consciously rejected common conventions in favor of developing a more comfortable or more meaningful approach to a specific aspect of ministry. They did not dismiss the importance of that aspect of outreach. Instead, they believed the same ministry could better be accomplished through a different approach.[4]

To experience the renewing work of the Holy Spirit in our ministries we need to be willing to try new "wineskins"—new methodologies, structures, and approaches. By studying the trends of the day, we can effectively present the changeless message of the Gospel to the people who need it most in a way they can understand.

Learning to Be Teachable

Approaching life as a learner creates the perspective for growth. The privilege of youth ministry is growth. If we are teachable, we interpret all of life's situations and experiences as opportunities for learning and personal involvement.

This perspective liberates us to view failure as an opportunity to learn. Since youth work isn't an exact science, a lot of what we do is a result of trial and error. We think that a pizza night with Christian videos would be a great idea so we try it, only to find out that on Friday nights most of the kids are working or out on a date. Be willing to try; the risk of experimenting is worth the possible failure if we are willing to learn all we can from it.

Some of the failures I made in the early years of youth work were my greatest teachers.

Six Mistakes I Made in the Early Years

1. *"Judging my value by the size of my youth group."* In those early days, my youth group of seven kids made me feel like I wasn't a valuable youth worker. I would easily get all seven in the church van and sheepishly drive to an event where some youth workers had two or three bus loads of kids. I felt small, insignificant, and embarrassed. "What kind of youth worker are you?" I asked myself. As I thought about it, I realized I was relational, humorous, practical, athletic, and liked to teach the Bible. I decided to focus these five characteristics on my seven kids. I learned that small is good because it is intimate, personal, more caring, and often has more impact than larger groups. Small is great too, in case you really fail—less people know!

2. *"Judging my impact by the response of the kids."* I had prepared what I thought was going to be a life-changing lesson for my magnificent seven. I had studied the Scriptures well and had memorized my lesson plan. I had developed creative learning activities and enthusiasm-inducing crowd breakers. I had even brought refreshments! The whole night was set up for significant life-change. Only one problem: nobody came! I waited fifteen minutes and began calling. I called the *whole* youth group and only got a hold of Chris; she said she'd be right over. Chris showed up. We ate cookies, drank red church punch, and I explained all the fun stuff I had planned. She looked at me compassionately and said, "I'm sorry no one else came. It looks like it would have been great, but can we talk about something that is bothering me?" Chris and I had a great two-hour conversation about some serious personal issues in her life. Ten years later we were reflecting on our old group and she said, "I'll never forget that night you dumped all your plans and helped me with my problems. I knew then that I was more important than your program."

People are more important than programs. It took the failure of a program to help me learn to evaluate my impact based on relationship, not the success of my program.

3. *"Thinking I could do it alone."* There was a time I tried to fix the van, drive the van, plan the games, lead the games, cook the meals, teach the lesson, and counsel the students. After a few retreats of flying solo I decided I needed to get help or quit youth work. I was young and energetic so I thought I could do it all. Later I realized that I couldn't do it all and that I was robbing others of their joy of participation and service.

Once I decided to involve others, I discovered they had been there all along. What had kept them from surfacing? My attitude. When we are young and insecure we are tempted to build the youth group around us. Many young youth workers fall into the Pied Piper syndrome. They like to solo on their float and have a parade of children follow them. Being a Pied Piper works for fairy tales and parades, but it is a lousy model for youth ministry.

Another reason why we find ourselves alone in youth work is that we are afraid. We may be afraid of losing control, or afraid of other adults. Some youth workers are comfortable with youth, but not with other adults. This doesn't mean they are a good youth worker—it means they haven't learned to relate with other adults. In fact, their inability to relate well with other adults hinders their impact on teens because they don't provide a positive model of adult relationships.

I discovered that others were willing to help me in our youth work. All I had to do was ask. Mr. Botham was a retired mechanic who had come from Sweden years ago. He had worked on the great Swedish ships and ocean liners. "Mr. Botham, would you be willing to be the mechanic for the church van? I don't have the time or the skills," I sheepishly asked. "Shoor, Shoor sonny. Dat would be no problem." replied Mr. Botham. For years he kept that old GMC van in running condition. I was relieved, and so was the church board and the parents.

Sue attended college out of town but came home every weekend. She was considering helping on our youth staff but didn't think she had anything to offer. "I'm shy and I don't know the Bible that well. I like the kids but I don't know how I can help." "What do you like to do?" I asked. "I like to ride horses, cook, and organize things," she replied. "How would you like to help me with the food for our retreats and events?" I asked (with a sense of urgency). "I'd love to do it!" she exclaimed. I was relieved, affirmed, and excited all at once. Relieved, because I hate buying food, organizing it, and cooking it. Sue loved to do this, she even *enjoyed* washing dishes and cleaning up! I felt affirmed because the Spirit of God was calling people to be a part of our ministry by using their strengths and gifts. I also felt excited because I began to understand that I didn't have to do it all. In fact, others were excited to help me!

Later on, Sue organized regular horseride Bible studies. They would ride to a lake, have a Bible study, swim, and ride back. She was working in her area of giftedness and God blessed it!

Thinking I could do it alone led to failure, but it also led to an influential lesson: "Learn to lead with your strength and staff to your weakness." I had made the pleasant discovery that I could minister with the things I did well and look for people to complement my weakness.

4. *"Not trusting anyone over thirty."* I began youth work in the early seventies. There was an atmosphere of suspicion between my generation and the "old fogies." I helped contribute to this alienation by avoiding interaction

with parents, keeping the youth group out of the mainstream of church life, and not recruiting staff over twenty-five years old.

My suspicion and distrust kept me and my youth group from growing. A lack of trust guarantees an atmosphere of stagnation. Later on, I learned that parents aren't the enemy, that the youth and church benefit by interaction, and that staff over twenty-five have much to offer. I learned that parents are far more committed to their kids growth and well being than I was as the youth pastor. I learned that youth enjoyed being with the adults in the church if it was a properly designed event. I discovered that my most faithful and effective youth workers weren't the cool college types, but those older. In fact, some of the most effective staff have been parents or grandparents who have already raised their kids. "Not trusting anyone over thirty" indicated that the problem was with me, not with those who had lived longer than me.

5. *"Being relational with no goal in mind."* In the early days of youth work I wanted to show the kids that I was cool, that I understood them and could relate. I was one of them. This was easy to do because I was ministering as a part-time youth director and was only two years older than two of the seven kids in my group. I had picked up from Young Life the motto "Earn the right to be heard" and took it to an extreme. "Earning the right to be heard" doesn't take a year before you mention God or personal spiritual issues. I learned from this mistake that I was operating out of a fear of rejection. "If I tried to deal with serious issues they might not come to the group," I thought. Or worse, "They might reject *me!*" I reasoned. Hanging out, but not moving forward in relationships isn't healthy for the youth worker or the students. I realize that now, but it took an angry senior named Steve to help me see my failure. "How come you never correct us or offer us guidance? I could really use some direction, or someone to kick me in the tail and say 'get going!'" he admonished.

As I thought about my passiveness I realized that I was timid and that was not a quality of spiritual leadership. Steve's admonition, along with God's word, helped me learn the lesson that we need to be both relational and intentional.

> For God did not give us a spirit of timidity, but a spirit of power, of love and of self-discipline (2 Timothy 1:7).

6. *"Not challenging students to serve or lead."* Because I was more concerned with being liked than being a leader, I seldom challenged my students to serve or lead. I challenged them to study the Bible, to pray, and to come to youth group, but I hadn't yet learned the value of "praxis"—the art of practicing what you have learned. I taught a lesson on servanthood but didn't of-

fer them an opportunity to serve. I encouraged them to study the Bible but never put them in a position to hold them accountable to do it. When I think of it, I may have been more harmful than helpful to their spiritual journey. They had learned from me–their youth pastor, that Christianity is something you know, not something you do.

I was quick to respond to their felt needs ("Let's go water skiing"), was learning at college about their prescribed needs, but hadn't become aware of their real needs. Robert was the intellectual in the group. He helped me discover my lack of challenge, "How long do you think it takes before we're ready to do something about what you've been teaching?" asked Robert.

"A little longer?" I sheepishly responded.

"I was ready six months ago. It's not that complex. If all we do is sit in here and talk about it, we'll never really learn it. Kids need to do stuff if they are really gonna learn it," explained Robert.

I sensed some impatience in his voice. I knew he was brighter than the average bear, but I also knew he was right. It was time to move on. It was time to challenge the troops to move out. I called the whole group together for our first "leadership meeting." Six out of seven showed up. Those six will lead the other one, I reasoned. At that meeting I said, "For too long now I've been doing the talking and you've been doing the listening. It has been suggested that we now start to let you talk more and do more. What do you think?" My new leadership "team" responded with enthusiasm; they decided we needed to have more discussion and less lecture from me. They picked one student to help lead the discussions by having him lead a small group (3–5 people!). They each decided what they could do:

• Steve would clean up the youth room and get some kids to help paint it.

• Chris would be the liaison between her Campus Life club and our youth group so we would be able to access all the events they were offering.

• Robert would research options for service projects.

• Robanne would see if she could get her dad to donate some furniture from his store for the youth room.

• Rochelle would ask her mom if we could have weekly meetings at her home (they had the nicest pool!).

• Roger asked his dad about getting free tickets to a baseball game for the whole group and friends we'd invite.

I sat there dumbfounded. There had been more energy and motivation in that room than in six months of youth work. They were fired up and ready to go. I realized then, that I had failed to understand that most teens are looking for a challenge to lead or serve, all we need to do is offer them choices.

Out of that first meeting, we acquired a redecorated and furnished youth room. We went to monthly events all planned by Campus Life (we rode in our faithful van). We began simple service projects like visiting convalescent homes, and taking food and clothing to Mexico. Parents began to offer their homes, pools, food, RV's, and cabins for the youth group's use (all we had to do was have a student ask). We also went to a bunch of Padre games (thanks Roger!).

Steve, the guy who was 'volunteered' to help lead the discussion group liked it so much he continued it in college. Steve did such a good job with youth that I delegated the junior high group to him and he led it with a passion. Today he is in his fifteenth year as a youth pastor. The privilege of youth work is the fruit. I'm grateful to have "stumbled" on the need to challenge kids to serve and lead. It brings me great joy.

> I thank my God every time I remember you. In all my prayers for all of you, I always pray with joy because of your partnership in the Gospel from the first day until now, being confident of this, that He who began a good work in you will carry it on to completion until the day of Christ Jesus (Philippians 1:3-6).

We have a window of opportunity to become relevant to the youth of our culture. According to Barna's research, most youth consider Christian churches in their geographic area to be irrelevant to the way they live.[5] The older they get, the less likely they are to consider the claims of Christ. The time to act is now. All growth involves change, and all change is risky.

> There is a time for everything and a season for every activity under heaven . . . a time to plant and a time to uproot . . . a time to keep and a time to throw away (Ecclesiastes 3).

We live in an age of cataclysmic change. But instead of denying it, we need to seize the day and see change as an opportunity rather than an opponent. Young people are searching for what most youth groups are offering. We need to build bridges into their world, so they can find it.

The bond we share today with the people of the past millennial eras is the sense of living in a time of enormous change. The last time the U.S. experienced such a deeply religious period was during the nineteenth century, when the country's economy changed from agriculture to industry. When people are buffeted by change, the need for spiritual belief intensifies.[6]

Discussion Questions

1. Discuss the contrasts of "The way it was—'70s" with "The way it's going—'90s" from pages 26–27.

2. How do these changes create the potential for more effective youth work in the future?

3. George Barna states, "Today's young people are quality driven." How have you experienced this in your youth work?

4. Do you think most students are looking for something more meaningful from a youth group? Why or why not?

5. Which of the "Six Mistakes I Made in the Early Years" (pages 27–35) do you most closely identify with?

6. Considering the trends of today, how can we become more relevant to youth in our area?

NOTES

1. Howard A. Snyder, *The Problem of Wineskins* (Downers Grove, IL.: InterVarsity Press, 1975), 122.

2. Ibid., 113.

3. George Barna, *User Friendly Churches* (Ventura, CA: Regal Books, 1991), 125.

4. Ibid., 172-73.

5. George Barna, *What Americans Believe* (Ventura, CA: Regal Books, 1991), 187.

6. John Naisbitt and Patricia Aburdene, *Megatrends 2000: Ten New Directions for the 1990s* (New York: William Morrow and Company, Inc., 1990), 271-72.

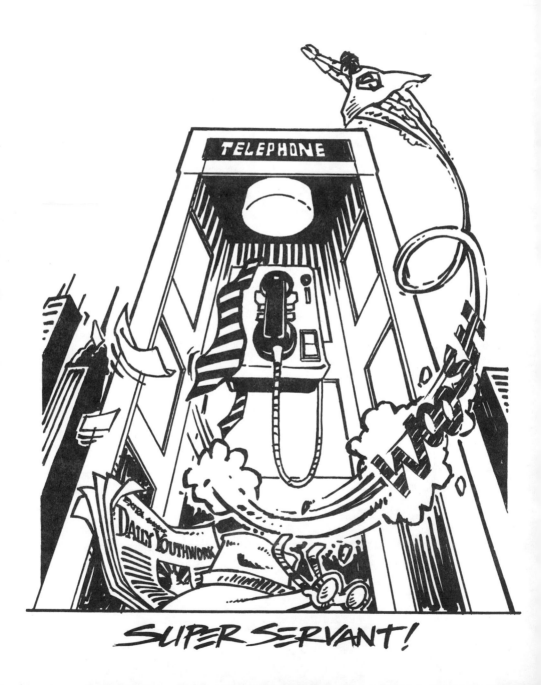

SUPER SERVANT!

The Way Up Is Down

Habit #2—"Effective Youth Workers
Are Service-Oriented"

That's a nice fluffy bun!" I thought to myself as I bit into my seventeenth Big Mac for the month. I am amazed at the consistency of quality McDonald's maintains across the country and throughout the world. As I sat there, in my yellow plastic chair, doing research on quality service, it occurred to me that McDonald's really pursues excellence because of:

- consistency
- cleanliness
- friendly service
- quick response
- value

As I thought about these qualities, it reminded me that these are also hallmarks of effective youth ministry. McDonald's knows these are crucial if they are to be effective in hamburger sales. They know their customer. They know that their customer wants to be able to go into any McDonald's and count on these qualities. Consistency helps build customer confidence and customer loyalty. If customers are loyal, they will return for repeat business. Selling one hamburger isn't as important as gaining a repeat customer.

McDonald's also knows that cleanliness is important because it makes their store distinctive. It used to be that hamburger joints were greasy and rundown. McDonald's introduced an industry standard for cleanliness that was quickly adopted by other fast food franchises. You can count on their stores being clean and friendly. If you step up to the counter to order you will be greeted by a smiling, neat, uniformed employee who cheerfully asks, "Welcome to McDonald's. May I have your order, please?"

McDonald's isn't just friendly, they are user-friendly. You can spot the golden arches at a hundred yards, even if you are going 55 mph on the freeway. When you walk in the restaurant, you feel comfortable because it looks familiar: the floor plan, decorations, menu, and uniforms all look like the McDonald's back home. You haven't been greeted yet, but you feel welcome. When your kids see the Playland, you become a hero for taking them to a "fun place to eat."

If you are in a hurry, McDonald's responds to your need in record time. You can zip through the drive-thru and be on your way faster than you can get a snack at home during a commercial. They don't offer everything, but you can count on getting what they do offer quickly and with remarkable quality. They have defined their niche and developed excellence in offering their service.

Value is one of the distinctives of McDonald's. You can buy a tasty burger for the price of a side order at a coffee shop. People eat at McDonald's because they can afford to and they get good food. It may not be gourmet, but at least the kids like it. In five minutes you can have a spread laid out for you and the kids, and have it cost just a little more than cooking at home; plus there is no cleanup or dirty dishes!

Ministry should be like McDonald's—consistent, distinctive, user-friendly, responsive, and valuable. We should be close to the customer—real close.

A simple message permeates the atmosphere. All business success rests on something labeled a sale, which at least momentarily weds company and customer. A simple summary of what our research uncovered on the customer attribute is this: the excellent companies *really are* close to their customer. That's it. Other companies talk about it; the excellent companies do it.[1]

Ministry is meeting needs. To meet people's needs we need to be close enough to know what those needs are and how to meet them. The Bible tells us that a good shepherd knows his sheep (John 10:14). He knows their peculiarities and particular needs. He can tell by the slight limp of a lamb that she might have a stepped on a burr. He can glance at the flock and know who is missing. He knows which ewe is pregnant and in need of extra food and water. He also is alert to the one sheep who is characteristically late and often left behind because he is a straggler. A good shepherd knows his sheep and they know his voice. Being close means not only knowing our sheep but letting them know us. Effective youth workers are service oriented because they are sensitive to needs, user-friendly and responsive.

Youth workers can learn something from well-run restaurants like McDonald's. We learn about service and teamwork from Ray Kroc, the founder of McDonald's and former owner of the San Diego Padres.

A well-run restaurant is like a winning baseball team. It makes the most of every member's talent and takes advantage of every split-second opportunity to speed up service.[2]

You may not think of yourself in the service business, but you are. Youth workers are in a service business of offering grace and truth to young people. It is our aspiration to make the most of every student's potential. We don't have much time with students, so we need to be quick to respond. We have limited opportunities to impact the students God has entrusted to us. To maximize these opportunities, effective youth workers have discovered the secret of being a servant and by empowering youth through serving.

Four Ways to Empower through Serving

1. Effective youth workers know how to build *significance* into serving. They create a vision that gives students the feeling of being at the center of something meaningful and necessary.

Joey was a timid and withdrawn student in our youth group. He came occasionally, but not enough for us to really get to know him. One time I gave him a ride home and asked, "What do you like to do?"

"Ah, not much. I like playing battle games at the park at night. But not too much else," replied Joey.

"Would you like to go to Mexico on a mission and help me with the games? I could use someone to keep the kids busy in the afternoons—you know soccer, piggybacks, and volleyball?" I asked.

"Sure, I'll do that," Joey promised.

I was surprised he agreed that easily; but he went. When we crossed the border, Joey changed—he went from shy, withdrawn, and passive, to outgoing, loud, and active. He was on a mission. He spent each day in the village actively playing with the kids for six or eight hours a day. When we'd return to our campsite, he'd collapse, totally exhausted. Mexico changed Joey because it made him feel significant; it gave him an opportunity to serve, and his contributions were valued. The children in the village loved Joey because he would play with them, wrestle with them, and tickle them. Many of these children had never felt the attention or affection of a man. Even though Joey was only fifteen, he met a need in the lives of these Mexican children. I asked Joey why Mexico meant so much to him.

"In Mexico I feel important because I can give something those kids need—attention. My parents are divorced and I never got any attention from my dad. I know how much kids need it. Playing with those kids is my mission. I just gotta do it."

Mexico was so important to Joey that he has gone back six times. We empower our students when we give them opportunities to gain significance through serving.

2. Effective youth workers understand the importance of *competence* and are committed to developing it in themselves and their students. Competence is a key element to empowerment. This doesn't meant perfection, but a commitment to growth and learning on the job. Empowered youth workers can look at a failure and ask, "What can we learn from this?" Competence involves risk and the possibility of failure, but always in the environment of developing. High standards of performance are reached when people have a sense of mastery over lower standards and feel successful enough to reach for the more challenging standards. In Joey's case, I helped him plan the games that would be appropriate for the Mexican children. I had been there and knew what would work. Joey was responsible to obtain the recreation equipment and ask for volunteers to help. This was a challenge to him the first year, but he was competent. The second trip he initiated higher standards for recreation and needed very little help from me. Joey felt competent and it empowered him and our Mexico mission to new levels of effectiveness.

3. Effective youth workers understand the value of *community*. Community is a sense of reliance on one another toward a common cause. If the common cause is service, there will be an environment for significance, competence, and community. Many youth groups fail to develop community because they don't have a compelling cause. Being together to be together is not enough; but "going to Mexico to love the children and tell them of Jesus' love" is a compelling cause.

Erin was having a difficult time breaking into our youth group. She said the group was "cliquish and not interested in me." She took a risk and joined our choir and drama group and went on tour. She said, "I'll give this group one last chance to see if I can feel accepted. If it doesn't happen on this tour, I'm going to another church." On the tour the focus became service and ministry. They traveled from town to town, singing and performing to hundreds of people. At one small town, she and a friend were asked to go sing to a dying woman in the hospital. She went, and halfway through the song she was overpowered by the dying woman's tears of appreciation. She realized that she was offering words of grace and truth to this woman—they were words of hope and significance. God was using her! Her focus shifted from potential rejection to being a significant part of a team. Needless to say, Erin discovered the value of community.

4. Effective youth workers have discovered that *fun* is a key ingredient to empowerment. Fun creates energy. Some of the most festive times I've had have come in the midst of challenging circumstances.

After a day of draining ministry in the deserts of Mexicali, Mexico we were starving, thirsty, and not interested in going back to the camp for cafeteria-type food. I pulled the bus into my favorite taco stand and announced, "We're going to ditch the evening meeting and dinner, and eat here. I want everyone to try a taco. I'll buy the first round!" I spent fifty dollars that night on tacos, but we sat there for hours laughing, drinking gallons of Pepsi, and seeing how hot we could handle our salsa. We were warned by the camp leaders not to eat in these stands, but I knew Lupe made the best tacos in the valley and I asked God to heal the tacos so we wouldn't get sick. The kids enjoyed the comfort of the restaurant after eating outside for days. The relaxation and the stories seemed to recharge our spirits. That night at the taco stand we discovered many funny and interesting things that had happened that we wouldn't have had time to hear if we had gone back to camp for the usual late night meeting. Building community takes time to laugh together. It usually helps to have food around too. Empowerment towards service grows out of an environment of enjoyment. Service doesn't have to be a burden we endure; it can be an opportunity that inspires us.

Youth work is more than meeting needs, it's also enjoying each other and sharing fun times together. Youth will feel significant if we begin with activities that are meaningful and make them fun. Almost any project or experience can be made fun. You have to look for it—kind of like finding a taco stand, at night, in the middle of the Mexican desert.

Being Environmentally Aware

An effective servant is aware of his surroundings. He knows what the available resources are and even anticipates the needs of the one he is serving. He is alert to his environment. To be effective in youth ministry we need to be aware of the environment. We need to realize that students are at different levels of spiritual interest. Our high school pastor, Dan Smith, uses four levels of awareness to help his leaders understand the multi-level environment of students.[3]

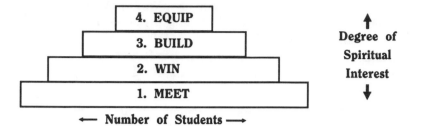

At the "Meet" level it is our goal to contact as many high school students as we can. We have an annual Spirit Night when we invite the cheerleaders from each of the local schools to compete (with the help of other students cheering) for spirit. We meet 1,000 students by offering this annual contact opportunity. There is no prayer, or anything religious, though we do host it at our church. Our goal is to be sensitive to the unchurched student and the school administration, at the same time letting them know that "Calvary Community Church cares about high school kids."

The "Win" level seeks to segue students from the Meet level into an opportunity to win them through relationship or shared experience. We offer fun, non-threatening activities that students who are seekers can participate in. Campus Connection is one of these events; it is a regular outreach designed for unchurched students to be brought by kids in the youth group. It is at this level that we seek to win the students to a personal relationship with Christ, or at least to consider the journey of faith.

Once students feel safe at the "Win" level they may opt to come to a "Build" level event which is our weekly Tuesday small group discussion and Bible study. Here they get to know a staff person and develop relationships with other students by discussing relevant subjects and seeing how the Bible addresses them.

The "Equip" level is designed to disciple the more mature Christian students through student leadership, service projects, missions trips, and ministry with our youth choir and drama team. This level is often forgotten, but is crucial. Many of the more mature students will leave a group or lose interest if they aren't challenged at this level. The "Equip" level is the most opportune level to develop service-oriented students. Evaluate the ministries you are offering your students. If they are all at the lower two or three levels, you are not challenging your students at the level needed to be effective in challenging each kind of student in your group. To ignore any one of these levels is to ignore students in your group.

Our aspiration is to build a ministry that is environmentally aware by ministering to students at each of these levels. Notice that the higher you go the less students are involved. This is the principle that Jesus experienced; I call it the "Free Lunch Factor." When Jesus offered to feed the 5,000 a free lunch, they hung around. When He asked them if they would follow Him, it narrowed down to 100. We know He spent much time with His faithful band of twelve, but when it came down to it, He was the most intimate with two or three. The higher the commitment, the less people will follow. Still, Jesus was available to people at all four levels of following.

Your perspective may keep you from ministering to one or more of these levels of kids. It's important that you evaluate your assumptions about the people you serve. Here are some typical assumptions:

1. Teens need to be entertained.
2. Teens don't want to be challenged.
3. Our teens don't have non-Christian friends.
4. Everyone in our group is a Christian.
5. Teens would rather play than serve.

If these are your assumptions about youth ministry, they will shape your programming. How you look at something and give order to it is called your "paradigm." It is a way of giving order and structure to our perceptions. Your paradigm will define your ministry. If your paradigm includes the five assumptions listed above, you won't feel any need to have events that are attractive to pre-Christian students. You also will not feel the need to develop "Equip" level events to help your students experience ministry opportunities and service. Chances are, you will be working with a small group of Christian students who are in cliques and don't get along.

To be effective servants/youth workers we need to examine our paradigms. To help you do this, consider the following questions:

1. What has been successful in the past? Are we a slave to it?
2. How has our student population changed? Have we adapted to it?
3. What needs exist now that didn't used to? What can we do about them?
4. What area would reap the greatest results if we gave it a little more attention?
5. What today is impossible to do, but if you could do it, would fundamentally change what we do in youth ministry?

These questions will help you draw outside the lines. One of my favorite TV commercials is the Isuzu Rodeo one where the teacher is saying, "Color inside the lines, the lines are our friends. Stay inside the lines." The camera pans to a woman driving a Rodeo on a road, quickly she smiles, and with a look of abandon and excitement she has a paradigm shift and careens off the road, "outside the lines," shifting into four-wheel drive for a blaze of off-road thrills.

We need to draw outside the lines if we want to see the world anew. We need a paradigm shift from what youth ministry was to what it can be. Someone once reminded me, "Your past success guarantees nothing." In fact, your successful past may block your vision for the future. Sometimes our pride gets in the way of what God wants to do in our youth ministry. That's why it is crucial to stay humble, stay flexible, stay open, and responsive—be a servant!

Eight Ways to Serve
1. Return all phone calls within 24 hours.
2. Call students for no reason, just to say "hello."
3. Inform the parents completely of all details for camps.
4. Take at least one student to lunch each week.
5. Do more listening than talking.
6. Go to the student recitals or events that few people attend.
7. Spend time with youth volunteers.
8. Drive students places.

Discussion Questions

1. Do you think McDonalds is a good model for youth ministry? Why?

2. What does a youth worker do to be close to his/her "customer"?

3. Describe various youth activities that are designed to be environmentally aware: meeting needs of students at different levels.

4. What do you think about the five assumptions that are discussed on page 47?

5. What need do our kids have that, with a little of our attention, would reap the greatest results?

6. What today seems impossible to do, but *if* we could do it, would fundamentally change what we do in youth ministry?

7. Discuss the "Eight Ways to Serve" from page 48.

NOTES

1   Thomas Peters and Robert H. Waterman Jr., *In Search of Excellence* (New York: Warner Books, 1982), 156.

2   Ibid., 255.

3   Dan has adapted this from training he received at courses sponsored by "Son Life".

CHAPTER FOUR

Power Surge

*Habit #3—"Effective Youth Workers Radiate
the Positive Power of the Holy Spirit"*

I opened the refrigerator and stared at the chilled leftover lima beans—they were bleached, pale green, wrinkled, and smelled bland. I popped one in my mouth but tasted nothing; I felt the fibrous texture, but the flavor was gone. It was an empty experience. Hoping for something nutritious and appetizing, I encountered pale, tasteless, bland lima beans. Then it hit me; I know some human lima beans! Cold, pallid, bland, and boring people. Some people are like leftover lima beans—they have become the frozen chosen! Instead of being alive and enthusiastic, they are lifeless and stagnant. They lead lives of quiet desperation, they are like a Pepsi that has lost its fizz.

Effective youth workers have discovered the secret of enthusiasm. You can be enthusiastic even if your aren't a twenty-two-year-old aerobics instructor. Youth work can be extremely draining emotionally and physically; but the secret of enthusiasm is not a physical one, it is a spiritual principle.

For the kingdom of God is not a matter of eating and drinking, but of righteousness, peace and joy in the Holy Spirit (Romans 14:17).

In youth ministry we don't simply build youth groups; we build the kingdom of God. The kingdom of God is where He is King and rules in honor, glory, and majesty. Sometimes we get trapped in the methodology—the "eating and drinking" of youth work, and forget the spiritual—the power of the

Spirit. Enthusiastic youth workers have discovered how to radiate the positive power of the Holy Spirit.

The word "enthusiasm" comes from the Greek words which mean to be "filled with God." To be genuinely enthusiastic means to be motivated, controlled, and influenced by God. It means that:

- Things that excite God excite you
- God's values become your values
- Things that please God please you
- Things that displease God displease you

Enthusiasm is more than an external shell of inspiration and hype. It is an outward expression of something good on the inside. It looks good on the outside because it's right on the inside. Enthusiasm can be a mark of God's ownership—it shows that we belong to the risen Christ.

Several years ago we were developing a list of the qualities we wanted to see in our student leaders. We decided we wanted our leaders to be F.A.T. Not fat, but F.A.T.—faithful, available, and teachable. We began to define and describe what we meant by each of these characteristics. After months of developing our student leader team, we still felt like something was missing. We had faithful student leaders—they completed their tasks and were responsible. They were available and spent much of their time serving their peers. They also were teachable and dutifully took notes and maintained their ministry notebooks in a way that helped them learn and grow. But there was still something missing. I'll never forget that "a-ha" moment I had one afternoon, as I talked with some adult leaders. I asked, "What's missing from our student leaders? They are F.A.T., but it's not enough."

One youth worker replied, "There isn't the power or the excitement."

"Yeah, that's it!" offered another. "They need to use the Force." (Star Wars was big then.)

"ENTHUSIASM!" I shouted. "That's what we're missing. They are faithful, available, teachable, and boring! These kids need to discover the excitement of living on the edge by being under the power of the Holy Spirit. We need to have FATTY leaders—F.A.T.E. and the E is for Enthusiasm! What good is it if we have solid leaders but their lives don't reflect the power and the mystery of God?"

I began a study of enthusiasm, and discovered that to impact people for Christ we need to understand and apply the principle of Spirit-empowered enthusiasm. Can you think of a person who radiates the positive power of the Holy Spirit? What impact did they have on your life? Recently, I asked these questions of my staff. Each person could cite a person who had left an impact on their life because they were radiating the positive power of the Spirit.

> May the God of hope fill you with all joy and peace as you trust in Him, so that you may overflow with hope by the power of the Holy Spirit (Romans 15:13).

When a person is under the influence of the Holy Spirit others will notice it. The early church was able to select leaders based on this observable quality.

> Brothers, choose seven men from among you who are known to be full of the Spirit and wisdom (Acts 6:3).

> When a person is under the direction of the Spirit, there will be supernatural results. These don't come from mere human effort, or positive thinking, they are a gift of God's grace made evident in our own lives (Galatians 5:22-25).

We aren't supposed to let wine or anything influence us. We are to be under the influence of the Holy Spirit (Ephesians 5:18). When we are under the Spirit's control we experience His power, joy, and enthusiasm. The effect is noticed by others and God.

> Because anyone who serves Christ in this way is pleasing to God and approved by men (Romans 14:18).

What a compliment, to be pleasing to God and approved by people! That is a desirable goal. Youth are looking for joy—they know happiness is temporary. They are desperate for peace—they often come from battles at home. Youth are also starving for hope because the world seems so gloomy. They are looking for choices in a world with declining options and longing for a certain degree of power in their lives. Hope, joy, peace, and power are the aches of adolescents in this age. A youth worker empowered by the Spirit can effectively model a life that reflects these qualities.

The Personality Myth

We live in a culture that is enchanted with externals. Popularity, possessions, status, and personality are the standards by which we measure ourselves. This enchantment makes it difficult to consider the internal energizing of the Holy Spirit. It seems so mystical, so subjective, and maybe spooky. After all, we are talking about a spirit. As a result of being bewitched by the externals we find it very easy to emphasize personality rather than character.

Shortly after World War I, the basic view of success shifted from the Character Ethic to what might be called the "Personality Ethic." Success became more of a function of personality, of public image, of attitudes and behaviors, skills and techniques that could lubricate the process of human interaction. This personality ethic essentially took two paths: one was human and public relations techniques, and the other was positive mental attitude.[1]

In our culture, people are rewarded for personality more than character. In fact, in some cases, if you are a person of character you will be punished. Consider the "standard operating procedure" of some businesses which bend the ethical line to maximize the profit margin. If you are a person of honesty and other positive character traits, you may find yourself in conflict with the corporate culture, you may lose financially, socially, or vocationally. There has been a shift in what our culture considers successful. In an era that barks, "Image is Everything!" it's easy to get lost in all the hype and gloss.

Prior to World War II we considered personal character a building block for success. Qualities like honesty, integrity, humility, courage, loyalty, justice, patience, industry, simplicity, modesty, and the Golden Rule were the hallmarks of effective living. One word which sounds archaic is "temperance" which means to forbear, abstain, and exercise restraint and self-control. This concept is so foreign to us in our age of excess that we have forgotten what it means. Yet in days gone by, temperance was an admirable trait of a person with character. Now such a person would be dismissed as prudish or not politically correct. The shift from character ethic to the personality ethic has led us to be a people with a craving for image. Status, reputation, and position now determine worth. It's not *who* you are, but *what* you have. The personality myth teaches that the goal is to be liked, so do what it takes to be liked. This obsession on externals forces us to focus on what we *do* rather than who we *are*. It makes us vulnerable to the opinion of others, and often compels people to strive to earn and achieve so they will have the goods which will proclaim their worth. If our basis for self-worth is the personality ethic, we will be very insecure because our security will be determined by the shifting perspective of others. The personality ethic, is weak because it is afraid of adversity, because adversity may challenge the source of worth. Therefore, I'll do anything to maintain the facade, lest I risk being exposed as simply a player in the Age of Flash.

The most tragic effect of the personality ethic is that it confuses the goals. The personality ethic says that the goal is to be liked. The character ethic says that the goal is to be like Christ. If a youth worker is operating on the personality ethic for self-worth, she may be tempted to do some things which may be unethical or ineffective, but will gain in her popularity. If her goal is to be like Christ, she will have a mental picture of what she should do even if it may not be the most popular option.

The character ethic realizes that God develops character in the lives of His people who are open to the reforming power of His Spirit. This relationship with God is critical for character development. Oswald Chambers reminds us of this truth.

We must never allow anything to damage our relationship with God, but if something does damage it, we must take the time to make it right again. The most important aspect of Christianity is **not the work we do, but the relationship we maintain** and the surrounding influence and qualities produced by that relationship. That is all God asks us to give our attention to, and it is the one thing that is continually under attack.[2]

We have had a shift from principles to popularity, from absolutes to relative options, from character based self-worth to personality based self-worth. This shift could be called a "paradigm" shift. Paradigm is from the Greek word, "paradigma" which means "a pattern or map for understanding and explaining certain aspects of reality." It's how you look at the world. We have had a paradigm shift from character-based ethics to personality ethics. If a youth worker is influenced by the subjective ethical environment he will believe that the most important aspect of his Christianity is the work he accomplishes, not the relationship he seeks to grow and mature with God.

My team and I have contrasted the personality ethic with the character ethic. We have developed the following chart that helps us see the implications for principle-based ministry.

Personality Ethic vs. (Basis for worth)	Character Ethic (Principle based)	Implications for Ministry
Goal: To be liked	Goal: To be like Christ	I don't have to base ministry on people's reaction to me. It should be based on helping others and myself become more like Christ.
Focus: Do/Actions	Focus: Who I Am	I need to be concerned with my growth as a person, not the jobs I do.
Depends on other's thoughts	Not interested in popular opinion	Do what I know is right even if it's against popular opinion (Colossians 3:23).
Strives to earn and achieve	Realizes God gives character	To build God's character in my life and not striving to build my personal success.
Exclusive	Anyone	All of us have the opportunity to be Christ-like.
Quick to obtain	Slow process of growth	Important things will take a lot of time. I must learn patience.
Play the fool to maintain	Not dependent on success	I must be driven from the inside out, not the outside in.
Quick to lose	Strong in character	God wants to build things into my life that can't be taken away by anyone else.
God may take reputation away to build character	God will not take character away to build a reputation	God looks at the heart, not appearance!
Afraid of adversity	Survives adversity	See adversity as a way of life, a way for God to work and build character.

As we discussed these competing ethical systems, we became aware of some fairly serious implications for our respective ministries. We realized that if we genuinely desire to see the mighty hand of God on our ministry, than we better make sure that we don't program Him out of our ministry, or worse, out of our personal lives. We eagerly anticipate the majesty and the mystery of God at work. For us it meant giving up some control to the Holy Spirit to make sure that there was room for Him to move. It meant scheduling our events a little looser, it meant being patient with gaps, and allowing the element of surprise to be a welcome guest rather than a frightening intruder.

Effective youth workers know that sometimes the best youth ministry occurs when we are dependent on God. Maybe we were interrupted in preparation and don't really have the Bible study down, yet God moves in a miraculous way. Maybe a student comes with a huge burden and commands the attention away from what you had planned to his issue. In both of these circumstances we are faced with abandoning or adjusting our plans to accommodate a situation we had not planned on. This is often God at work. He doesn't phone ahead to tell us what He's doing. He doesn't schedule an appointment, "I'll be at youth group Wednesday, and I'll move in a mighty way. Can you give me thirty minutes?"

I have noticed that God often works best when I am experiencing what I call "Divine Irritation." I know it's supposed to be Divine Intervention, but it sometimes seems more of an irritation to me because it effects my plans. I am the master of my youth group, the skipper of spirituality, the captain of the ship, what I says goes; then God decides to cut in on my turf, I get irritated. I have actually thought, "What is He doing here?! I didn't plan for this!" It's at these times that I realize how insecure and weak I am. I am using the youth group to fuel my personal needs because I have bought into the personality myth. My focus has shifted from "What does God want to do?" to "What will make me look good?" or "What do I want to do?" I could pity in my weakness but I realize that my weakness is an opportunity for God's strength.

> In the same way, the Spirit helps us in our weakness. We do not know what we ought to pray for, but the Spirit Himself intercedes for us with groans that words cannot express. And He who searches our hearts knows the mind of the Spirit, because the Spirit intercedes for the saints in accordance to God's will (Romans 8:26-27).

Effective youth workers radiate the positive power of the Holy Spirit even when they are tired, weary, or feel useless. We are able to do this because the energy doesn't come from ourselves—it comes from the dynamic of the Holy Spirit within us. The Spirit is the energizer.

Late Night Cookies and Milk

We had been sleeping on the floor of a church classroom for five nights. Forty of us in one room—guys on one side, girls on the other. The snoring and other "night noises" were keeping me awake. As a veteran youth worker, I had learned to sleep lightly so I could discern any late night activity. My trained senses were working against me now; I craved sleep, I was exhausted.

By day, we were youth on a mission—seeking to help establish a new church in a town 100 miles from ours. It was hot, fatiguing work. I was usually the last to go to sleep and the first to wake up. Five hours of sleep per night wasn't enough to keep my flesh from kicking in. I was irritable, and began questioning why I had come on this "stupid mission." Sure I was the youth pastor, but why can't we go where they have beds? I pondered. I couldn't sleep so I glanced around the room. I noticed that Kevin was awake and looking straight at me. "Are you awake, Kevin?" I asked.

"Yeah, I can't sleep. You too?" he replied. He seemed much more alert than I.

"Too much noise, do you want to go in the kitchen and get a snack?" I heard myself say. I couldn't believe my own words! Why was I all of a sudden gracious? *I want my rest, I deserve my rest, I can talk to Kevin tomorrow,* I reasoned.

"Talk to him now," came a voice inside my head.

"I don't feel up to it, I'm too tired and cranky," I protested.

"I will give you strength," said the voice.

"I'll definitely need it. If you want me to talk with him, you will have to give me strength and alertness, because I don't have it," I explained.

"In faith, act like you are energized by me," said the voice. I stood and quietly stumbled into the kitchen. By the time I had poured a glass of milk and grabbed the cookies, I was totally awake.

Kevin began, "I really needed to talk. I just can't sleep. I need to talk with you about my dad. I'm really worried about him and I have never told anyone about this. Can we talk?"

I sensed God's presence in that room, and I then realized He was the voice that had been speaking to me. As Kevin talked, I felt the positive power of God's Spirit begin to radiate within. I noticed I could listen and concentrate on what he was saying. My body no longer felt tired, I didn't need to sleep. Kevin opened up to me that night at a level which was very meaningful to both of us. It launched us into a close and significant relationship—one I would have missed if I had tried to relate to him in my strength.

Because that night I didn't have it, it all came from God. I was empty, and yet God used me. I learned that night that God uses our weakness to build bridges into the lives of other needy people. He uses our emptiness as opportunities to fill us with His grace. He uses our weariness as a backdrop for His mighty power, as he uses our dullness to awaken us to something much more conscious of the genuinely important.

My grace is sufficient for you, for my power is made perfect in weakness. Therefore, I will boast all the more gladly about my weaknesses, so that Christ's power may rest on me. That is why for Christ's sake, I delight in weaknesses, in insults, in hardships, in persecutions, in difficulties. For when I am weak, then I am strong (2 Corinthians 12:9-10).

Discussion Questions

1. Who stands out in your mind as being "enthusiastic." What kind of impact did they have on your life?

2. How do we as youth workers struggle with the personality myth? How does the motto, "Image is everything," affect us?

3. How do you feel about Oswald Chamber's words, "The most important aspect of Christianity is not the work we do, but the relationship we maintain"?

4. Discuss the contrasts between the personality ethic and the character ethic and the implications for ministry (page 58).

5. Which one of these issues is a struggle for you?

6. Describe a time when God came through for you—when you experienced His strength in the middle of your weakness.

NOTES

1   Stephen R. Covey, *The 7 Habits of Highly Effective People: Powerful Lessons in Personal Change* (New York: Simon & Schuster Inc. 1989), 19.

2   Oswald Chambers, *My Utmost for His Highest* (Grand Rapids, MI: Discovery House Publishers, 1992) Oswald Chambers Publications, August 4 Devotional, Emphasis added.

Empowered toward Excellence

Habit #4—"Effective Youth Workers
Believe in Others (and Their Growth)"

Youth workers are people with vision. Who else would look at a twelve-year-old boy who is being obnoxious and disruptive and believe someday God is really going to use him? Vision is faith in action, it's seeing what could be. It's not allowing our present parameters to determine our future horizons.

Rod was one of the most hyper junior high guys I had ever met. He constantly talked and always had some body part in continual motion. I dreaded having him in my cabin at camp because he never grew weary, in spite of that verse which says young men get tired. I was challenged by Rod to direct his enormous amounts of energy into something productive. I suggested long-distance running. He took it up, and before I knew it, he was running five miles a day. In high school he went out for cross country and became a star. He still was hyper at church, just a little more tired. I challenged him with being in student leadership, and he rose to the occasion and became an innovative, energetic leader in our youth group. One of his ideas was to play Ultimate Frisbee (frisbee football) at 10,000 feet on our backpack trip in the High Sierras. It was a lot of fun playing on the tundra, someone would run for the frisbee and then disappear in a hole of chilly water. If you fell, it didn't hurt because of the mossy, grass-like carpet we were playing on. It probably killed the plant life and upset the ecological balance of the area, but it was a blast. We were playing for the championships—my team against Rod's. I had the Frisbee and he was guarding me. The game was tied 1–1, and we only had a few minutes to play. I spied my team-member open in the end zone and forcefully snapped the Frisbee to him. Rod was guarding me close and my hand caught him right in the nose and broke it. Rod bent over in pain and cradled his broken nose. I felt terrible. I wanted to be able to stay ahead of this kid, but not break his nose!

We grabbed some snow from the ice pack and placed it on his swollen face. I called the game, but Rod wanted to finish it. As we limped back to camp he joked with "how competitive I was that I would break a kid's nose just to win." Then I realized why I believed in Rod—he was a lot like me. I saw in Rod the potential to be an effective leader. He had courage, was persistent, self-disciplined, energetic, playful, and willful; he'd make a perfect youth pastor! I believed in Rod and his growth, he wasn't perfect, but he was always in process. He seemed to have an accurate understanding of his strengths and weaknesses. Like me, Rod was often criticized for being too rowdy and too radical. Today he is an effective youth pastor to a large youth group in southern California. He's still rowdy and he's a radical for God. I thank God that He gave me the vision to see what Rod could be.

Effective Youth Workers Are Visionaries

Vision is a specific mental image of what God wants to accomplish through you to build His kingdom. This is my working definition for vision; let's take a look at some of the key words. Vision is "specific." Vision is not some vague idea of what you wish for, it is a detailed picture of what God wants to do. Vision is "mental"—it requires imagination, concentration, and focus to develop a vision. Vision is an "image"—not a foggy, sketchy, impressionistic rendering, but a clear, definitive, objective portrait of what God seeks to do in the lives of people. Vision comes from God. God supplies the vision.

God's plans for this planet are too important to tolerate human-generated visions and schemes. God places His vision within the leaders He has chosen and gifted. Not every Christian has vision, but every effective Christian leader has vision.

Vision is not simply some song from Don Quixote about "dreaming the impossible dream," but dreaming the most possible dream. It is rooted in reality and then figures in the exponential factor of God-at-work which leads to supernatural results. There are at least three factors to understand about vision:

1. Vision is specific
2. Vision is people-oriented

3. Vision positively embraces the future

Vision Is Specific

To lead people, a leader must have an idea of where he wants to go. A visionary youthworker has a specific mental image of a possible and desirable future for his youth group. A specific vision is essential because it defines the future state and defines believable steps on how to get there. A specific vision motivates because it describes a condition that is better in some important ways than what now exists. A visionary youth worker provides the essential bridge from the present to a preferred future for the youth.

Mark Weston knows what he wants. As a junior high pastor, he has defined his "Profile Characteristics" of what he wants a student to be like after spending two years in the junior high group. This becomes the vision of the entire junior high team. They use it to plan retreats, weekly programming and individual discipleship. Not every student reflects these characteristics after being in the group, but many do. Much more than if Mark didn't define specifically what he feels a discipled junior high student looks like. Specific vision motivates and it guides. God can work in dramatic ways even with junior high students, and within the brief two years!

Vision Is People-oriented

God's kingdom is built by people. He is a lover of people. His vision always involves His desire for people. God's vision will always involve how He can use you to change the lives of people—the kids in your youth group. This is a priority—programs are important, and buildings are helpful, but the vision involves life-change in people. If vision is people-oriented, then we must consider the felt needs of those we seek to serve and lead.

When the organization has a clear sense of its purpose, direction, and desired future state and when this image is widely shared, individuals are able to find their own roles both in the organization and in the larger society of which they are a part. This empowers individuals and confers status upon them because they can see themselves as part of a worthwhile enterprise.[1]

When young people understand they are a vital part of the vision, they gain a sense of importance. Effective youth workers help their youth capture the vision, whether they be the youngest junior high student, or the most mature high school student—there is a consensus of what is important in our youth group.

Great leaders often inspire their followers to high levels of achievement by showing them how their work contributes to worthwhile ends. It is an emotional appeal to some of the most fundamental of human needs—the need to be important, to make a difference, to feel useful, to be a part of a successful and worthwhile enterprise.[2]

Vision is important to people because it meets some of their most basic needs of security, belonging, and significance, as well as challenging them to invest their lives in something of unparalleled importance—the kingdom of God.

Vision Positively Embraces the Future

Vision always involves risk. Risk is an inherent part of vision because of the change required to reach the vision. Vision refuses to be content with the status quo. Vision also refuses to be intimidated by the uncertain future. Instead of hiding from the future, a visionary will embrace it with confidence, knowing that the embrace will help shape the future. Leaders are only as powerful as the ideas and vision they communicate. If they embrace the future with confidence and a passionate image of what can happen, people will follow. To be effective youth workers we need to be visionary leaders—out in front, thinking ahead of our youth and helping them determine the future by building faith today.

Leaders, in a special way, are liable for what happens in the future, rather than what is happening day to day. This liability is difficult to measure, and thus the performance of leaders is difficult to measure. Though we do need to review past results and processes, the emphasis on the duties and performances of leaders has to be on the future. It is especially hard to remember that today's performance from a leader succeeds or fails only in the months or years to come. Much of a leader's performance cannot be reviewed until after the fact. Today's trust enables the future. We also enable the future by forgiving the mistakes we all make while growing up. We free each other to perform in the future through the medium of trust.[3]

Vision is compassionate, it doesn't force people to stay stuck, but allows them the freedom and the space to change. It is the expectation that God will use us in the future in spite of our present weaknesses.

> Being confident of this, that He who began a good work in you will carry it to completion until the day of Christ Jesus (Philippians 1:6).

Paul exhibited vision when he penned this verse. He expected God to continue to work in spite of present circumstances. Paul was in prison when he wrote this and had every reason to be negative and pessimistic. Instead, he was hopeful and expectant. He could picture from his cell a "specific mental image of what God wants to accomplish through his friends to build God's kingdom." Paul provides us with an excellent example of vision. Vision is one way we see faith in action. Being a leader means challenging the inhibitors

of God's vision. Vision builds on the past, but focuses on the future. It anticipates that God will be at work in ways we can imagine and in other ways we
could never dream of. Vision empowers God's people emotionally and spiritually to move forward in faith.

Communicating Vision

Growth is more likely to occur in youth groups where there is a specific de-
scription of what they are trying to accomplish. Clear, effective communication helps people understand the vision and helps them own it. If vision
describes a desirable change in the future, it implies growth. A well-stated,
understood vision statement creates expectancy—people expect that something is going to happen. Youth typically don't value routine and predictability, they like things to be dynamic and innovative.

When vision is understood and owned it creates momentum and a feeling
of accomplishment. Maybe nothing has actually happened yet, but people
feel a sense of accomplishment because, "We are in this thing together and
we expect something to happen."

Teri was struggling with her youth group. She asked to talk with me after
I had spoken at a youth workers convention. "I don't know what it is, I just
feel bored with my youth group and they act bored with me," she explained.

"What is it that you are trying to accomplish?" I asked.

"What do you mean?" she asked with a quizzical look.

"What are your goals; what would you like your youth group to look like
after being with you for three years?" I inquired.

"Well, I'm not sure. I guess I have just tried to entertain them, and keep
them out of trouble. I'm not sure they are ready for a challenge," Teri reasoned.

"Your lack of challenge is why you and they are bored. It could be so pre-
dictable coming to youth group that kids come expecting it to be dull.
Growth is never boring. Describe in writing what you'd like God to do in the
lives of your kids, share this with them and ask for their help. I predict that
you'll have an exciting group in one year if you do that."

A few years later I encountered Teri and she told me what happened. "I
left the convention determined to share my vision. I realized I had been
afraid of sharing my vision. I had it all along, but I thought the kids would
alienate me if I shared it. Instead, they became motivated when I shared my
dream for a loving, caring, active group which meets needs of people in and
outside the group. We've taken trips to Mexico; urban trips, and they are
even gearing up for the most frightening outreach—to their campus! It's re-

ally true, 'without vision the people die' and our youth group was dead, now it's alive!"

I smiled and asked, "Was there a cost to communicating the vision?"

"Sure, at first some of the kids didn't like the seriousness of our discussions and they stopped coming. But most of them came back around when they saw what we were doing was really significant and fun. All of a sudden it was cool to care; it used to be cool to be cold and rude."

"How did you communicate your vision?" I asked (always looking for new ideas).

"We wrote a vision statement which captured in a sentence what we wanted to develop in our group. We wrote it on a large sign and hung it on the wall in our youth room. It was more than a slogan because the students helped write it. It took a long time and involved a lot of students, but now they own it. We studied several verses until we came up with a statement that we all felt called to, challenged by, and one we could own. Our group has doubled in size in two years and it's definitely not boring," beamed Teri.

Teri had learned the habit of communicating vision. She discovered that vision is the base for the identity of a youth group. The vision helps define the culture of a youth group—it sets the tone for how we work together and what we attempt to do. God supplies the vision. Teri had it all along, and she needed to let herself see it. Fear often keeps us from seeing the vision that God has for us. Fear is the enemy of vision, it is a result of a loss of control or balance in our life. God seeks to give us a spirit that will fan the flame of our vision.

> For this reason I remind you to fan into flame the gift of God, which is in you through the laying on of my hands. For God did not give us a spirit of timidity but a spirit of power, of love and of self-discipline (2 Timothy 1:6-7).

VISION

Power _____ Love

Self-control

I see vision as a balance between power and love. If we are afraid, we lose self-discipline and become defensive. Instead of being self-disciplined, we are self-protective. This is out of fear and keeps us from understanding the vision God has for us. But God's spirit is a spirit of power balanced with love. At times we will need to ask, "What mighty work does God seek to do through us which is totally impossible unless He chooses to work?" This is power vision. The other side of the balance is love vision. It involves asking, "Who needs to experience God's touch of love, healing, and grace?" God has already placed the gift within every believer, it's not our responsibility to fake the gift but "fan into flame the gift" God has placed into us.

Don't fake it—fan it!

Focus Shift

Sometimes our focus intimidates us. What we are looking at scares us into inactivity and timidity. We need to shift our focus. We need a paradigm shift from:

Program to people

Production to principles

Past to future

Obstacles to opportunities

Fear of criticism to cultural relevance

An insecure person often concentrates on the wrong things. If we are going to challenge youth with a vision of significance and community, then we will need to look past our program into the eyes of the people we work with. We will need to focus more on principles and less on production. We might need to take some time out to think and reflect and actually **not do** something. A principled paradigm realizes that behavior and potential are two different things. As a result, the principled youth worker refuses to judge, label, categorize, and stereotype people. He sees within each individual the limitless capacity of God's grace. A principled youth worker doesn't have to overreact to negative behaviors, criticism, or human weakness. He understands that potential is a process, not a point. As a result of this liberating perspective we can visualize growth and potential in others. We begin to look more into the future and less into the past for our significance. Pity the youth worker who judges his worth on the last big success he had.

Opportunities surround the visionary youth worker—some call them obstacles. But the opportunist understands them to be stones which will become stepping stones and later milestones. Many youth workers get stuck in the fear of criticism—some real, some imagined. It takes courage to be relevant to a changing culture. It's safe to maintain a "sanctification mindset"—which says, "Let's not be too relevant or else we'll be too worldly and become tainted." There's risk in reaching people with needs. But then again, why else would they need a Savior?

It was in the early days of punk. I was a youth pastor at the Evangelical Free Church in Fresno, California. It was a conservative church in a conservative town, and there was a conservative church board who kept an eye on things. I liked the refreshing honesty and angst that was common in punk, so I invited a new, cutting-edge Christian band to do a Wednesday night concert.

Okay, so Wednesday was a bad night to choose; it was Family Night. We had Awana Club for kids, choir, a variety of classes for adults, our youth programs, and of course the church board meeting. I made some flyers and we spread them around town, we were expecting 200 students but over 800 showed up! I guess this neophyte band, Undercover, was a draw! You should have seen the eyes on the Awana kids when the parking lot turned into purple mohawks on parade!

The church board members were not amused when they heard the intensity and volume of Undercover. They heard the concert, even though they were four buildings away. Parents thought that the youth group had gone to hell on a skateboard when they dropped their kids off for youth group. I never knew we had that many punks in Fresno. We had a few in the youth group, but who would have guessed there were hundreds?

That night, more than one hundred kids responded to Joey Taylor's offer of salvation—most of them kids we'd never reach with our preppie program. I received enough complaints to wallpaper my office with phone messages and letters. But I learned a lesson that made it worth it all—being culturally relevant requires courage to take criticism. That was the beginning of a long string of concerts.

Focusing In

Since it is impossible to meet all the needs of youth in your community, you need to decide which needs you will meet. You can ask yourself: What needs am I burdened with? Which are we uniquely qualified to meet? What might our niche be? Which of these needs of youth in our community make me pound the table with passion? Then ask yourself, Why do we exist? What is our mission statement? To help you in this process, look at the diagram on page 75.

This is a planning tool I use to communicate vision, and develop goals for our ministry with my staff. I start from the top and work down. After we have determined our PURPOSE, we need to ask ourselves how we are different from other youth groups in town. For us, we are "Christ-centered, biblically based, culturally relevant, and outreach oriented." This is quite different from other significant ministries in our area, but it is us, it is our DISTINC-

TIVE. Under OBJECTIVES we are looking for broad categories of ministries we know we will always do. For instance, Bible study, evangelism, caring, discipleship, etc. We then seek to visualize our vision and describe it in writing as our DREAMS. We then record our steps toward the dreams as our GOALS.

The Calvary Rocket planner is only one way of taking the vision and implementing it. Vision is a specific mental image of what God wants to accomplish through you to build His kingdom. We need tools like this to build. We also need a team of builders.

The Empower Team

Vision is crucial if we are going to be effective in youth ministry. But we can't do it alone, we need to have a team that empowers each other towards excellence. I'd like to offer "Eight Goals for an Empowered Team of Youth Workers":

1. Expect the best from your staff
2. Know the needs of your students and staff
3. Establish high standards of excellence
4. Learn from failure
5. Promote team spirit (minimize competition)
6. Encourage and model personal renewal
7. Celebrate achievement and growth
8. Balance ministry with the rest of your life (able to say "no")

So from now on we regard no one from a worldly point of view. Though we once regarded Christ in this way, we do so no longer.

> Therefore, if anyone is in Christ, he is a new creation; the old is gone, the new has come! (2 Corinthians 5:16-17).

Discussion Questions

1. How have you seen potential in a student before they discovered it in themselves?

2. "Vision is faith in action, it's seeing what could be. It's not allowing our present parameters to determine our future horizons." Why would vision be essential for effective youth work?

3. Discuss why these three factors are necessary for vision:

   Vision is specific.

   Vision is people-oriented.

   Vision positively embraces the future.

4. Why are leaders liable for what happens in the future?

5. Discuss the "Calvary Rocket" on page 75. How could you utilize this planning tool for a current youth ministry?

6. Develop some practical steps of applying the "Eight Goals for an Empowered Team of Youth Workers" (page 73).

NOTES

1   Bennis, Warren and Burt Nanus, *Leaders* (New York: Harper and Row Publishers, Inc., 1985), 91.

2   Ibid., 93.

3   Max DePree, *Leadership Is an Art* (New York: Dell Publishing, Inc., 1989), 114–15.

THE CALVARY ROCKET

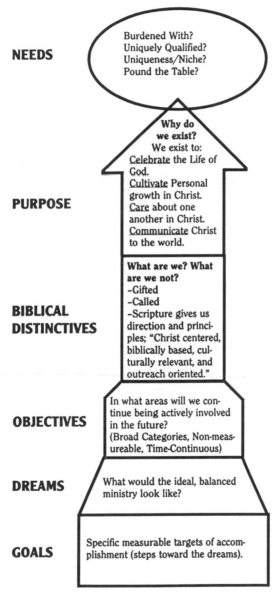

NEEDS
Burdened With?
Uniquely Qualified?
Uniqueness/Niche?
Pound the Table?

PURPOSE
Why do we exist?
We exist to:
Celebrate the Life of God.
Cultivate Personal growth in Christ.
Care about one another in Christ.
Communicate Christ to the world.

BIBLICAL DISTINCTIVES
What are we? What are we not?
–Gifted
–Called
–Scripture gives us direction and principles; "Christ centered, biblically based, culturally relevant, and outreach oriented."

OBJECTIVES
In what areas will we continue being actively involved in the future?
(Broad Categories, Non-measureable, Time-Continuous)

DREAMS
What would the ideal, balanced ministry look like?

GOALS
Specific measurable targets of accomplishment (steps toward the dreams).

CHAPTER SIX

The Balancing Act

*Habit #5—"Effective Youth Workers
Lead Balanced Lives"*

What kinda pop, man?" asked the Caribbean store keeper.

"What kind is there?" I replied, hoping for something new.

Pepsi, Marinda . . . Pepsi," he said as he fished his hand around the cooler's melting ice water.

Two choices—Marinda, which is an orange-flavored soda, and the old standby, Pepsi. I was thirsty for a Mountain Dew, but on Roatan Island we were lucky to have chilled Pepsi. Every afternoon, after I had taught school, taken my siesta, and coached soccer, we made our pilgrimage to the store. I was disappointed in the lack of variety, but there was something comforting about the ritual. We would ask for something, the store keeper would say he didn't have it, we'd buy something else and leave content. The natives of Roatan didn't have much, but they were content. After 365 such episodes it was time to return to California. Culture shock was worse coming home than going overseas. My first trip to the supermarket threw me into a panic: Pepsi, Coke, Dr. Pepper, root beer, 7-Up, orange, AND Mountain Dew! Too many choices! I was overwhelmed by the toilet paper aisle, mountains of T.P. with variegated colors, sheets, plies, and textures. On Roatan we were happy to have the rough, tan stuff that resembled plywood. I was stressed by the choices. I was psychologically fatigued by the options presented to me. I was on overload, and I was only shopping.

As we sprint toward the year 2000 most of us live in a continual state of choosing. Life becomes a multiple-choice test. Even television was simpler when all we had to watch were the three networks. Now, with cable our options are well over 100. It takes so much time, energy and focus just to make it through the rudimentary choices of the day.

Upon returning to California, I was concerned with the waste going into trivial decisions. It seemed that people were stressed by the pace of life and were on decision overload. I longed for the simple days on the island where life walked slow enough to chat with the folks and sip a Pepsi.

Pace and product are the beat of the day. Our culture attaches value to a busy person—they must be important. Achievement is another source of affirmation in our culture. "Just Do It" is more than a slogan for shoes; it is a national creed. Consequently, we begin to believe we need to hurry up and do more.

Pressure comes from a society that values **being hurried.** We have grown accustomed to having everything NOW. We are the instant generation. We like to tell a sign behind a restaurant what we'd like for dinner and then expect the people inside to have it prepared by the time we pull our car around to the serving window. Automatic teller machines give us instant cash. Microwave ovens give us immediate meals. Modern malls give us sudden debt. We have a love affair with haste.[1]

Being a youth worker in the age of haste is challenging. We tend to react in one of two ways. On one hand we have "911 Nancy" who responds at all hours to all calls for help. She is a seven-day-a-week-youth worker. Her husband and children will just have to understand she "is doing God's work, they can wait." At the other extreme is "Phil Family Man." He announced to his church, "I can only be out two nights a week. My first priority is my family." Phil had heard this idea at a conference and decided to try it out. It did give him more time with his wife and infant son, but the youth group suffered from his lack of availability.

Nancy and Phil illustrate the pull towards polar extremes when we lose the balance in our lives. Paul Borthwick offers three areas that need balance if we are to be effective:[2]

1. Personal time vs. ministry time.
2. Thought time vs. activity time.
3. Time with adults vs. time with students.
    I'd like to add a fourth:
4. Time with parents vs. time with youth work.

Personal Time Pressures

I didn't used to struggle with the tension of personal time vs. ministry time, and that was a problem. If something needed to get done, I'd carve out time to do it. That time came out of my personal time. At one point I was working seventy hours a week, teaching junior high, high school and college twice a week each, attending games on Fridays, youth events on Saturday, numerous meetings all week and feeling pretty positive about myself. I was important because I was busy. I was valuable because I produced. "Who else could teach three different lessons to three different age groups in three consecutive hours every Sunday? I am capable and worthwhile," I told myself. I missed countless quiet evenings with my wife. "There's the Lock-in," I protested. My daughter's first words were uttered while I was gone. "We always go to Mexico for a week. It's crucial, it's a mission," I rationalized. My wife and I had issues to face and conversations that needed to take place, but I didn't have the time. I was too busy.

I used to think I was running TO something, but I was running FROM something. I was staying so busy because I thought I needed to succeed; I was running from failure.

In high school and college I was a runner. If I wanted to compete faster, I ran harder and longer. I learned that to win you need to work harder and faster. I applied this philosophy to youth ministry and it got results.

My youth group grew to numbers in the hundreds. People affirmed me for the results. Our youth group gained a very favorable reputation in the city. People offered to be on staff; I had a waiting list. Church members offered us their cabins, boats, recreation vehicles, and Palm Springs condos. Many regularly donated money for our scholarship fund. The church leaders gave me a promotion, a larger office, and a raise. I was asked to write articles and speak on "The Elements of Successful Youth Ministry." Results—there you have it: I was a success. Or was I? Nobody, I mean NOBODY ever asked me, "Tim, do you think you are working too much?" or "How are things at home, are you balancing your time with your family?" Looking back it makes me fearful to see how imbalanced I was. It also makes me angry. Why didn't anyone say anything? Couldn't they see my life was out of balance? I was running harder and faster; I was still competing. Instead of the church braking me from my frenzied pace, they affirmed it. I needed a church leader to question me about my family life, but instead they applauded my productivity.

I've observed that sometimes churches do more to fuel compulsive behavior than heal it. It's a blurry line between biblical servant and codependent enabler. But it's nothing new. Since the exit from Eden, sin has refused to let us rest. Our frantic pace is a result of taking shortcuts in life. Sin is often masqueraded, but unmasked it's "the passion to have it all, now." Our natural drives lead us to an overloaded life.

We believe the lies that "Bigger Is Better" and "Worth Equals Net Worth" and "Busyness is next to Godliness." In order to feel better about ourselves, we spend more effort on our ministry. Meanwhile, our primary relationships at home suffer because of neglect.

Thought Time vs. Activity Time

Youth work creates a tension between being with students and being alone so you have something to offer when you are with them. We tend to favor one over the other: study time or student time.

Dave is a highly relational youth worker. He's got the trendy hair-cut, the stylish sports car, and dresses vogue. In a word, Dave is "cool." Most of his time is spent eating with kids, listening to CD's, going to concerts, or just "hangin'" with them.

Dave has a difficult time studying for the Bible study. He'd rather "be relational than academic." Balance for Dave is to read a Christian book for an hour every week, spend an hour studying the Bible, and an hour preparing the lesson. These three hours are difficult for Dave, but for him, it was the balance he needed. He asked a friend to hold him accountable for these three hours.

Julie is an analytical youth worker. She likes to study trends of adolescents and think about her particular students. She is most content reading a journal on adolescent behavior in her office. She likes to study, plan, dream, and think. She is a expert on the computer and creates some high-quality graphics with her desktop publishing. She maintains office hours from 9 to 5 and is there most of the time. If students want to see her, they can call and make an appointment. Julie needs to balance her thought time with some activity. She decides to spend three afternoons out of the office and go where her students are—at games, the mall, rehearsals and workouts, where they work and where they relax.

Adult Time vs. Student Time

Spending all of your time with students makes for a tired and immature youth worker. We need to be around other adults who will challenge us to grow and, in some cases, serve us. Youth workers who spend all of their time with students expose themselves to the risk of losing their balance and perspective.

Tom loved to spend time with guys in his small group. Since he was single, he spent every weekend with them. After awhile, I noticed Tom was beginning to respond like a teenager. He was having difficulty relating to his peers on the youth team and began to lose his objective perspective on the kids. One of the guys in his small group was developing a serious drinking problem, but Tom was defensive and made excuses for this teen. As a result of this imbalance, Tom began to lose credibility with the other adult volunteers and raise serious questions from parents of the guys in his small group. One parent pointed out, "It seems like Tom needs the students more than they need him." This sent up the flares for me. I got together with Tom, told him of the parent's comment and we developed a plan to balance his life. I asked him to spend two weekends a month and two nights a week with friends in the "Twenty- Something Singles" group. His friends were glad to see him back, and Tom discovered a sense of balance, perspective and freedom that he had lost. I asked some of the high school guys in his group what they thought about the "new Tom" and one of them said, "It's better now that Tom has a life!"

Of course, the other extreme is to be like Julie, and want to barricade yourself in your office or home and not spend time with students. When Julie began to force herself to hang out with kids she discovered a renewed understanding and empathy for kids that you can't get from a journal. Her youth group members introduced her to their friends and parents. She was able to teach more effectively because she could picture the world of her students with much more detail and understanding. Her credibility skyrocketed with the students because they sensed she cared.

Time with Parents vs. Time with Students
This never used to be a tension for youth workers—it was a given to spend the time with the kids. But now things are different. It used to be we would see kids come to youth group three times a week, plus weekend events. Those days are gone. Our time with kids has lessened. Many are too busy to come to youth group more than once a week.

How can we have an impact on a generation of busy kids? Spend time with their parents. If we can minister to their parents then we have increased the impact we have on the home. We have then acknowledged that our kids come from family systems and we are seeking to support and influence that system, rather than simply an individual in the system. Most youth workers are afraid of parents—they see them as problems, not people. They are afraid if they get involved with parents they will lose control of the youth group or the youth will feel betrayed.

Steve was a popular youth worker who had been at his church for five years. Some of the graduates had come back to help in the youth ministry.

They liked Steve and were glad to be back in the youth group—but this time they were staff. Steve had his standard annual parents meeting where he handed out calendars and coffee and discussed this year's schedule. That was his ministry to parents. He was afraid if he had more interaction with parents they would only have more opportunity to complain or criticize. He wanted to play it safe. He wanted to keep control. He wanted to keep his distance from parents.

Steve enjoyed working with his staff; he was older than them by only a few years. They liked the same TV programs as he did and tended to have the same style of humor—*Saturday Night Live* meets *David Letterman*. Youth ministry was fun, working with this gang.

After a while, parents began to question the "depth of his teaching" and the "lack of emphasis on discipleship." Mr. Major was a leader in the church and an adult Sunday School teacher. He was concerned that his daughter, Melody, was not involved with the youth group. He used to make her go in junior high, but in high school he felt she should have the choice. She chose not to go, and when encouraged to attend, she would respond, "The youth group is cliquish and Steve is boring." Mr. Major shared his concern with some other parents over coffee before Sunday School. Some of them had teens that didn't like coming to the youth group. The more they talked, the more critical and negative they became. Before they had finished their second cup of coffee some of the parents were thinking about replacing Steve as youth pastor.

Mr. Major scheduled an appointment with the senior pastor and shared his concerns regarding the "lack of maturity, depth, and breadth" of Steve's ministry. He told the pastor, "Several of us church members and leaders are considering leaving the church to find a ministry that meets the needs of our teens."

Pastor Warner had seen this type of spiritualized manipulation before and did not fall into Mr. Major's trap. "Have you talked to Steve about this?" asked Pastor Warner. "I'm sure he'd benefit from being aware of your concerns."

"No, we haven't," explained Mr. Major. "Isn't that your job?"

"The Bible says if you have a concern with your brother you need to go directly to him. I think you need to go directly to Steve. To avoid him is to promote discord and hurt the unity of the Body," admonished the wise pastor. Mr. Major reluctantly agreed to talk to Steve.

Steve listened to Mr. Major's complaints and asked, "Are you concerned with the spiritual maturity of the youth group?"

"Why yes," replied Mr. Major. "That's why I'm here."

"Then you would say we need to pray for these kids?" asked Steve.

"Of course, they need our support," agreed Mr. Major.

"Then would you be willing to help organize a Parent's Prayer Support Team for our youth ministry?" Steve inquired.

"Yeah, sure. What would it require?"

"I'll prepare a monthly prayer newsletter informing your team of the prayer requests and praises for answered prayer; you get together with parents to pray for our youth group, the staff, and me."

Six months later, Steve still had his job. He also had a team of fourteen parents committed to pray for him, his staff, and the youth. Steve discovered a principle for effective youth ministry: Involve the parents in what you are doing. Not only did Steve have a Parents Support Team (PST) but he also began to include parents in events, errands, and camps. They provided much of the labor intensive work that freed up the staff to be relational with the students. As parents barbecued hot dogs, they could observe their teens developing relationships with the youth staff. As the parents met together and prayed, they began to compare notes about their kids. Some of the kids had legitimate concerns about the youth group, but many of them were using the complaints to "get back" at their parents. They knew it would get a reaction out of their parents. Mr. Major, and other parents, told their kids, "The youth group isn't perfect, but it's our youth group and we need to support it. You need to go and give it another chance. Let Steve know what you think we can do to improve, and give him the opportunity to address it."

Parents and youth workers can work together. I'm finding out that a ministry to and with parents is essential. If we include parents, they tend to work with us, when we don't, they tend to work against us. Jesus said something about, "He who is not for Me is against Me."

Myths That Lead to Imbalance

I was presenting a parent's seminar in North Carolina. I was noticing the parents were beginning to fade and think about lunch, so I decided to recapture their attention. "We are going to break for lunch in a few minutes, but I want to warn you about the sweet tea (iced tea). During the break, I snuck over to the kitchen and poured eight ounces of poison into the five gallon container of sweet tea. Okay, now back to parenting. A myth is something that seems true but is tainted by a little falseness. It is mostly true, feels comfortable and familiar, but it has just enough false in it to taint the whole batch. A myth is like the sweet tea, it looks good, tastes good, but if we ingest it it will bring us trouble. Let's break for lunch. After we eat we will talk about myths."

At lunch a funny thing happened. The coordinator of the citywide seminar was sitting at my table, and as he reached for some potato chips he knocked over his sweet tea—all twenty ounces of it. People teased him about drinking the "poisoned cup." He claimed my story made him nervous; but he cleaned everything up, got another plate of food, sat down to eat, but noticed the centerpiece was out of place. As he moved it to the center of the table he knocked over a tumbler full of tea; it splattered all over me. Parents were rolling with laughter. The jokes and the teasing made it a very enjoyable lunch. I'm not sure those parents will remember the six hour seminar on parenting, but they will remember the story of the poisoned sweet tea!

Myths, to be dangerous, only need to have a little bit of falseness. If we place our confidence in something that is somewhat untrue, we have a shaky foundation. Let's take a look at these myths that lead to imbalance:

1. "Youth workers don't work with parents"

We have demonstrated this is a myth. To be effective with teens, we need to consider the family system they come from, and relate to that system.

2. "Earn the right to be heard"

I know this is a popular slogan for youth ministry, but it can be taken to an extreme. I know because I spent two years trying to be cool and build friendships before I ever mentioned God, let alone sin, or other serious topics. Teens want us to be relational, but they need for us to be intentional.

3. "Teens want fun, not substance"

This is mostly true, no teens want boredom, but most want significance. They are looking for credible responses to their question, "So what?" We have discovered it is a lot easier to begin with something that is inherently significant and add fun, than to start with something fun and seek to add significance.

Dewey Bertolini encourages youth workers to "Choose the activities based on the purpose. Do nothing without meaning." This purpose needs to be clear in all we do in youth work.

By establishing the purposes first and choosing activities based on the purposes, the following will result; you and the entire staff will feel a sense of achievement as you meet the clearly defined goals; you will experience the thrill of meeting specific needs in the lives of the young people; the young people will learn to discern and model our achievement orientation as they see a goal accomplished; the activity calendar will have a sense of balance since every event centers on a comprehensive list of purposes; you will have avoided the leading cause of youth ministry burnout—the expenditure of time and energy with nothing lasting to show for it; you will be following the most important programming priority: DO NOTHING WITHOUT MEANING![3]

4. "Act like one of them"

Teens are looking for someone who understands them, not acts like them. They want someone they can look up to, not across to. Many youth workers have mistaken being relational with being immature. They have believed the myth that says, "To relate to teens you must demonstrate teen-like behavior." Some teens have told me these are the youth workers they despise. Teens need models who walk ahead of them as guides in life. If they get too far ahead they are hard to relate to and keep up with. If they are playing around and getting lost on the journey, it doesn't inspire much confidence from the teens. Teens choose not to follow adults who act like adolescents.

5. "Relate and teach from your strength"

This has been a common maxim in ministry to utilize your strengths and staff to your weakness. In other words, do what you are best at and look for others to compliment your weaknesses. This may be true in staffing, but it doesn't work as well for spiritual growth. I used to think my youth group needed to see me as a spiritual knight ready and able to take on the dragons of this world. I wanted to present to them a capable, successful, strongman. But as I took a deeper look at myself, this wasn't very authentic. I struggle with insecurity, fear of rejection, and fear of failure. I realized I needed to share some of my weakness if I was to be genuinely authentic. As I began to experiment with relating from a point of weakness, it opened the hearts of many in the group. I'm learning when we relate and teach from a position of strength we often build barriers, but when we relate from a position of weakness, we build bridges into the lives and hearts of our youth.

6. "Don't show emotion"

This is similar to the previous myth in that it promotes being less than we really are. Somehow we have bought into the notion that the more mature we are the less emotion we show. We have wrongly equated the demonstration of emotion with immature behavior. Teens are emotional, and they are looking for adults who know how to deal with their emotions. Denying we have emotions like fear, doubt, anger, and sadness robs us of the opportunity to build bridges into the hearts of the teens in our group. I used to believe in the "don't show emotion" myth. I felt my youth group would feel I was "too weak" or "not a man" if I shared my emotions. Anger was the only emotion I felt like displaying. It's OK for a man to be angry, but to admit I was lonely or sad made me too vulnerable. I taught many fine lessons from the

Bible, but I don't think they impacted the youth. They were food for thought. My goal was to teach content, to help youth comprehend the truth of God's word. I prided myself in how we had progressed through the Old and New Testaments, and how the students had learned how to study the Bible on their own. But something was missing—the passion and the excitement were fading. A speaker said, "A lesson prepared in the head reaches heads. A lesson prepared in the heart reaches hearts. A lesson prepared in a life reaches lives." I realized I had only been preparing my head—my teaching was basically mental. I wasn't sure how to prepare my life to reach lives, but I decided to share my life as a part of my teaching—my struggles, my joys, my confusion, and my ambivalence. As I became more authentic about my emotions, my lessons became colorful. The hues and tints began to show. Before, I was teaching in black and white. When I learned to teach with emotion, I began to teach in color. I discovered you reach people at a much deeper level when you teach to the heart rather than to the head.

7. "Don't delegate—they'll blow it"

This myth is easy to believe because we have so much evidence and experience that it is true. But this myth will bring death to effective youth work. If the youth worker wrongly assumes she must do it if she wants it done right, she will be a very controlling and tired person. Ministry is about serving others—people grow best when they are serving. We need to share the serving so others can grow. Sure, they may not do it as well as we can—but the point is progress, not perfection. The wise youth worker knows what she can delegate and does so. She also works with a net. Just like a tightrope walker has a net underneath, so does an effective youth worker. We create a safety net to catch people when they fall. They will fail and will fall, but they won't be destroyed. People learn much from failing. We shouldn't rob them of the lessons that can only be learned from failure. But, as shepherds, we need to protect them from feeling like failures.

I have observed that students and staff are real teachable after they fail with an assignment. We don't need to fix blame, but we do need to learn from the failure. I tell my student leaders and staff, "If we can learn from it, it's not a failure; unless we try to blame someone." Taking a critical look at something and fine-tuning it helps us pursue excellence. But it takes failure to develop excellence. Mediocrity can happen without failure, but excellence takes risk. We empower people to serve when we trust them with the ministry. I like to challenge my team to entrust the ministry to student leaders. I tell them, "The same Holy Spirit that is in you is in them!"

The Rhythm Method of Youth Work

No, I'm not advocating a birth control schedule! I'm talking about the natural rhythms that occur in every youth group. The effective youth worker senses the rhythm of his group because he notices certain patterns. Nature provides us with many examples. The ocean tides go up and down each day. When the tide is high it's easier to launch a boat; when the tide is low, it's the right time to go skim boarding. The seasoned youth worker notices the tidal changes in his group. There will be times of high tide excitement followed by low tide blues. Knowing when to launch a ministry will be determined by the "tide" of your group.

Groups also have seasons. You may be experiencing winter with a frigid, unresponsive group who keep to themselves and don't venture out. Following your Easter Outreach trip you may experience a thawing and a rebirth into the spring. Students may show excitement in reaching out. In the summer of your group you may notice a desire for resting and building relationships. The autumn of your youth group may involve some changes. Just like leaves turn colors and drop, some of your leaves may change. Of course, these seasons of a youth group aren't necessarily connected to the four seasons, but in some cases they are. Study your group and see what types of natural rhythms it has. It will help you balance your ministry because you will discover "there is a time and a season for everything under the sun." An effective youth worker is balanced because he knows what season it is.

A balanced youth worker has developed a sense of equilibrium with his time. He has been able to reconcile the four major competitive time demands:

- Personal Time vs. Ministry Time
- Thought Time vs. Activity Time
- Time with Adults vs. Time with Students
- Time with Parents vs. Time with Students

Study the diagram on page 96, "Balanced Time = Effectiveness." Picture the center of the circle being horizontal and balanced on a pin—like a plate spinning on a stick. Youth ministry balance can be that tricky.

Evaluate your personal ministry balance by shading in each pie slice to the degree you spend time on that piece. For instance, if you spend a lot of time with students, then shade one of the pieces termed "students." Notice the corresponding balance to student time—it could be "Time with Parents" or "Time with Adults." If you spend time with your adults friends, then shade that piece according to your estimation. If you never spend time with the parents of students, leave that piece unshaded.

After you shade the pieces, you will have a graphic representation of how you spend your time. Evaluate if this time balance reflects your priorities; if it does, you now have a pinwheel that will affirm you. Each youth worker will have different priorities for time. There is no "right answer" for all youth workers. The point of the Time Pinwheel is to make ourselves aware of the competing time demands that exist in youth work and to see if we are balanced in handling them.

When you go to the medical doctor for a check-up he does a variety of diagnostic tests to see if you are healthy. Each person may vary in their response to the individual tests. Your resting pulse might be sixty-four beats per minute while another person's might be eighty-two. You both could be in good health, but many other variables need to be considered. A healthy body is balanced. A healthy youth worker seeks to maintain balance by holding himself accountable to a sensible pace and schedule.

The Personal Pathology of the Youth Worker

A sense of pace, balance, and accountability will help a youth worker stay healthy and effective. But what is it that causes many of us to "crash and burn"? I would like to suggest six common vices of youth workers. I call them the "Six L's Down":

1. Lack of accountability

I used to meet with Lee (not his real name) for lunch. We'd encourage each other in our youth ministry, trade ideas, and share resources. Occasionally we'd plan events together. Lee was an articulate, passionate, and dynamic youth pastor. He never told me he and his wife, Cherie, were having problems. By looking at them they had it all together—large church, new house, new car, healthy children, and an ample salary. People in his church were pleased with his effective ministry and were settling into the idea of Lee and Cherie being at First Church for a long time; but midway into his third year Lee was fired for having an affair with a woman in the church. The youth group was devastated, the church was shocked. Cherie was crushed beyond recovery—so she left Lee.

I was stunned by the exposé. I had no suspicion of Lee's adulterous behavior. I felt betrayed and angry. "How could he do this to everyone?" I wanted to know. Lee and I spent dozens of hours together—but not once did we ask each other any of the *hard* questions like:

"Are you in the Word?" "Do you have a heart for Jesus?"

"How are you feeling about God?"

"How are things with your wife?"

"Do you find yourself looking outside your marriage for satisfaction?"

"When was the last time you got away alone with your wife for a romantic weekend?"

"How can I pray for you, confidentially, about your marriage?"

"Have you benefited from marriage counseling?"

I didn't ask the hard questions, I didn't think about it, now I do. I don't think we can afford not to. The problem is we are *more comfortable in being peace-keepers than truth tellers.* We'd rather convince ourselves that we are "keeping the peace" by being superficial, protective, and avoiding accountability.

No one grows best where truth is absent. No one is pushed *to be* and *to do* the best. And when you look at this deficit from a Christian perspective, it describes a situation where men and women are neither going to become all that God has made them to be nor will they gather the spiritual energy or passion to make it happen.[4]

To become all God has intended for us to be means we need to be accountable for our balance of time and our personal purity and holiness. I've chosen to meet weekly with two mature Christian men who hold me accountable for the hard questions. I think they have helped me in a way I wished I would have helped Lee.

I needed an accountability partner. Someone who would ask me hard questions, keep me from bluffing, and hold my feet to the fire concerning my spiritual growth. Axiom: Spiritual health demands a friend who will walk alongside us, speak truth to us (even when it hurts), and keep us honest in our relationship with God and with other people.[5]

2. Loneliness

Rick is one of the guys in my support group. He was relatively new to our church when he walked up to me one Sunday morning and asked, "Are you lonely? Do you ever feel alone in your ministry?" I was taken back by his directness, but as I recovered I realized I had two options: (1) Pretend I wasn't lonely and deny it (as I had for years). "How could I be lonely? Thousands of people know me!" I rationalized. (2) Answer with authenticity and vulnerability. I heard myself respond, "Yes, at times I do feel alone. I'm surrounded by people, but it's always in the role as pastor, leader, or manager. I need to be 'just Tim.'" Because of Rick's courage, we now meet to deal with our macho tendencies to take on the world by ourselves. I suppose women can be macho too, but we should call it "macha"!

Sometimes the pretending isolates us.

Therefore each of you must put off falsehood and speak truth fully to his neighbor, for we are all members of one body (Ephesians 4:25).

3. Laziness

Youth work can be a haven for lazy people. Whether you are a volunteer or a full-time youth pastor—your work with students can be easy and relatively painless. I think youth ministry attracts lazy people. Where else can you claim to be a "professional" and daily wear shorts or jeans, get paid to go water skiing, to the beach, or on fun adventures? Sure, there is a lot of behind-the-scenes-work like—buying hot dogs, selecting sunscreen, and planning the recreation. But there is also a lot of unaccounted time which can easily be spent on things that don't impact the Kingdom of Christ. I know youth pastors that spend hours each day memorizing the sports page "so they can relate to the jocks in their group." I wonder if they have spent much time in the Bible—memorizing the box scores of the eternal conquest. I may sound critical here, but I'll admit my bias: I'm tired of our profession being relegated to the minor leagues of ministry status because youth pastors are perceived to be lazy or incompetent. I'm not sure if it's a perception problem, or a performance problem. But I get upset when someone says, "When you grow up and become a *real* pastor. . ." they must have some flakey, lazy, immature youth pastor in mind.

I'm not advocating becoming a workaholic, but some of us could use a little more compulsion for work. We only have so many opportunities to impact students for Christ. We need to maximize the opportunities God has given us—whether we're volunteers or full-time. We need to invest our available ministry time wisely.

Be very careful, then, how you live—not as unwise but as wise, making the most of every opportunity, because the days are evil (Ephesians 5:15-16).

4. Lust

In youth groups we talk to our students about lust, but we don't talk about our lust. We'll get together to talk about friends who have fallen in sexual sin, but we'll avoid sharing our own precarious struggle with sexual temptation. Maybe it's considered a taboo topic for youth workers. It seems inconsistent to talk with teens about premarital sex and personal purity, but have no dialogue with other youth workers about our own sexuality. Lust gains a foothold in our lives when we pretend we are exempt from it. The denial gives lust power. Bringing it into light causes it to wither, shrink, and lose its grasp on us.

Youth work can be a very sensual experience. Hormones are raging through the bodies of adolescents who are fascinated with their newly discovered sexuality. Many of them can't wait to try out their "new equipment."

Our youth may see us as adults who have become comfortable with our own sexuality. We have weathered the hormonal hurricanes of adolescence and settled into being a woman or a man. A person who is comfortable with their sexuality can be very attractive to a teenager. You may be the most attractive model of a male or female to a student in your group. That may fuel your ego—but it can also fuel your folly. Teens can become manipulative, seductive, and destructive with their sexuality. Others have been victimized by the lust of others—they live with the shame and pain. As their youth workers we need to model a healthy, pure sexuality to them. We can be authentic about sexual attraction, but we need to help them discover escape routes from lust. The best way to help our youth deal with lust is to model victory in our own lives.

I define lust as:

Living

Under

Sexual

Tension

Lust is a willful choice of allowing natural sexual attraction to get a grip on us and place us under sexual tension. Our focus becomes under the influence of our lust. Being in a youth group can be a dangerous place for a youth worker given to lust. But there is help for those of us who struggle with lust.

So, if you think you are standing firm, be careful that you don't fall! No temptation has seized you except what is common to man. And God is faithful; He will not let you be tempted beyond what you can bear. But when you are tempted, He will also provide a way out so that you can stand up under it (1 Corinthians 10:12-13).

5. Loser mentality

Feeling like a "loser" can cause a youth worker to lose her balance. This can be seen in two extremes: feeling "I can't do anything"; and feeling "I can do everything." Both imbalances are dangerous. The "I can't" youth worker won't take the risks inherent to youth work. Fearing failure and rejection, she'll play it safe—right down the mediocre middle. The youth won't be impressed, they won't be challenged, they won't remember their youth worker or the things she tried to teach.

The "I can" youth worker might be remembered; but he probably won't last as long; he'll burn out early because he tried to do it all by himself. His false confidence was really a mask for his personal insecurity. Youth workers like this are often called a "flash in the pan." The loss of ego balance can be disastrous for youth workers. If we think we are worthless, we may feel we have nothing to offer the youth. If we think we are God's gift to the youth group, our arrogance may alienate the youth we are supposed to serve.

One of the places you'll see a lot of strutting and masquerading is at youth worker's conferences. There is a lot of comparison and "group envy" as youth workers compare the size of their groups and budgets. The youth worker who is on stage as the one who is really "making it happen" may turn out to be next year's moral tragedy. I don't want to sound judgmental or harsh, but I have noticed a connection between pride and moral failure.

Super Stan

I was interviewing for a job at a church which had a growing reputation for being innovative and culturally relevant. They had several applicants from all over the country. It came down to me and another youth pastor who lived 1,500 miles from the church. I knew the church and the area, and was interested in the possibility of going there. I didn't get the job—they offered it to the other guy. The pastor told me they selected him because of his impressive accomplishments, national caliber, huge youth group, and dazzling denominational references. I was disappointed with the rejection, and began to feel like a loser. I thought I could do the job, I thought I interviewed well (all six interviews!). They told me I really understood their unique setting, but they chose the other guy! Why? I reflected on what the pastor told me; they had made their decision on different criteria from what they told me. They changed the rules in the middle of the game! Instead of looking for someone who could lead a balanced and effective youth ministry, they had hired a "big shot"—someone with a more impressive pedigree.

Now I was mad as well as sad. I felt the church had compromised on its standards. It bugged me so much that I called the pastor back and asked him to explain it to me again. "We chose Stan because of his ability to rally massive amounts of students and organize big events," explained the pastor. I hung up feeling like a big loser.

About a year later, the church fired Stan for immorality. Turns out he was lacking integrity in his sexual life as well as his ethical life. His proud accomplishments listed on his resume turned out to be grossly exaggerated. Some of the references were fabricated. I mourned for the pain and confusion of that youth group. I could picture their steely, gray eyes of disbelief and cynicism in the wake of this announcement.

My grief was deeper than the rejection I felt. Not getting the job made me feel like a loser; betrayal makes everyone feel like a loser. I learned a lesson from Stan: a lofty sense of self makes a precarious perch. Or, as the Bible says, "Pride comes before a fall." Stan felt so low about himself that he had to create a Super Stan. The fantasy may have gotten him the job, but it set him up for destruction. Our self-esteem needs to be shaped by who we are in Christ, not our accomplishments. It is His work at the cross that makes the difference, not ours. We can't really discover ourselves until we find ourselves in Jesus. It is His reputation that we need to be concerned with, not ours. Being made in the likeness of Christ means our identity is being shaped by Christ, not our personal ambition or agenda. It basically means letting go of the dying, temporary props for worth and embracing the living, eternal truths that shape us into Christ-likeness.

For to me, to live is Christ, and to die is gain (Philippians 1:21).

A friend of mine had a successful, long-term ministry at a large church. He developed a reputation of helping people discover their spiritual gifts and maximize them in ministry. A larger, prestigious church in another state recruited him to be on staff. He went to candidate and was impressed with the modern and large facilities, the ample budget, the large staff, and the wealthy, well-educated congregation. He took the position, but only stayed a matter of months. I asked him what happened, "They appealed to my pride. I didn't trust my gut feeling (which was negative), and my pride got in the way of making a good decision." As I listened to him, I made a mental note, "Don't let your pride make your decisions."

6. Last to have my needs met

This is the sixth 'L' that can ruin a youth worker. Youth ministry is very demanding. There is no end to the needs we are surrounded by. I'm not sure why you went into youth work, but I think a lot of us like to rescue people. We gain a sense of meaning and significance by helping youth. It's a fine line between compassionate youth worker and codependent enabler.

Rescuing a person from the natural consequences of his behavior enables him to continue in irresponsible behavior. Today we call a person who continually rescues another person a codependent. In effect, codependent, boundary-less people "sign the note" of life for the irresponsible person. Then they end up paying the bills—physically, emotionally, and spiritually— and the spendthrift continues out of control with no consequences. He continues to be loved, pampered and treated nicely. Favors and sacrifices are part of the Christian life. Enabling is not. Learn to tell the difference by seeing if your giving is helping the other to become better or worse. The Bible requires responsible action out of the one who is given to. If you do not see it after a season, set limits (Luke 13:9).[6]

It's easy to do "too much" as youth workers. That late night call from a teen may turn into an all-nighter. Our role as caregivers may blur into caretakers. The expectation then becomes, "No matter what the problem, you, as my loving youth worker, will take care of me." Sometimes, the most loving thing we can do as youth workers is to let teens experience the consequences of life.

Don't play the role of Rescue Ranger with your youth. It may make you feel important, but it can make them dependent and resentful.

Devon was one of the most popular youth workers I have known. The kids in our youth group followed him around like Pied Piper. Devon was single and had a cool apartment near the beach. He would often have a small group of teens over for dinner and then a game of beach volleyball as the sun set. Devon spent almost all of his free time with adolescents—they were his friends. He was there when Nick had his bout with crack; he helped Sally with her depression. Carol will always remember Devon's persistent care as she struggled with bulimia. Jimmy appreciated Devon's help in talking to his friends about their need for Christ. Wherever there was a need, Devon was there to meet it.

I'll never forget that breakfast with Devon when I stared into his blank, weary eyes. He wasn't his enthusiastic self. He normally was positive and energetic. Today, his empty gaze was a window to his soul. He was on "E", completely drained, emotionally "out of gas." I said, "Devon, you have given so much, there is nothing left for you. You were the last to have your needs met. It's time that Devon took care of Devon." He broke his fixed, glassy gaze and smiled, "I'm totally burned-out with nothing left to give, and I did it to myself. I'm such a dope—I should know better."

Devon took a sabbatical from youth work. He focused on the personal issues that made him a Rescue Ranger. Through Christian counseling, supportive friends, and accountability, Devon recovered his perspective, balance, and strength. He's back in youth work, but now he can say "no."

Discussion Questions

1. What do you think you would notice if you returned to our culture after being in a Third World country for a year?

2. Tim Kimmel says we are a society that values being hurried, and has a love affair with haste. How do you relate to this personally, and in your youth ministry?

3. Which of the four balancing acts do you find the hardest to balance?
   ☐ Personal vs. ministry time

   ☐ Thought vs. activity time

   ☐ Adult time vs. time with students

   ☐ Time with parents vs. time with students

4. Review the myths that lead to imbalance. What parts of them seem true? What parts are dangerously false? (pages 84–86)

5. Evaluate your personal ministry balance by using the "Time Pinwheel" on page 96. Shade the pie slices according to how much time you spend on that piece. Share and discuss your pinwheels.

6. Which of the six common vices of youth workers do you think is most destructive?

7. What are some ideas to counter these destructive habits?

Balanced Time = Effectiveness

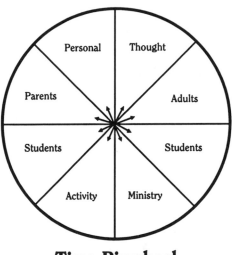

Time Pinwheel

NOTES

1.   Tim Kimmel, *Little House on the Freeway* (Portland, OR: Multnomah Press, 1987), 30.

2   Paul Borthwick, *Feeding Your Forgotten Soul—Spiritual Growth for Youth Workers* (Grand Rapids, MI: Zondervan Publishing House, 1990), 105–6.

3   Dewey Bertolini, *Back to the Heart of Youthwork* (Wheaton, IL: Victor Books, 1989), 146.

4   Gordon MacDonald, *Renewing Your Spiritual Passion* (Nashville, TN: Oliver Nelson, 1989), 186.

5   Paul Borthwick, *Feeding Your Forgotten Soul—Spiritual Growth for Youth Workers* (Grand Rapids, MI: Zondervan Publishing House, 1990), 167.

6   Drs. Henry Cloud and John Townsend, *Boundaries* (Grand Rapids, MI: Zondervan Publishing House, 1992), 85, 197.

CHAPTER SEVEN

The Big Adventure

Habit #6—"Effective Youth Workers
See Life as an Adventure"

Jesus challenged us with a call to adventure. He didn't say, "Take up your couch and follow me." He beckoned, "Take up your cross and follow me." He didn't promise miracles, an influential position, or wealth. He offered the unknown. When Christ calls people He doesn't offer a ten-year plan with benefits. He says, "Follow me." When Christ calls, He calls us from a life of comfort and certainty to a walk of challenge and uncertainty. A journey of faith involves risk. We have chosen to follow Christ, not because He has told us the details of what lies ahead on the journey, but because we believe in Him and trust His leadership.

When Christ says, "Follow me," He is asking us if we are willing to have an intimate relationship with Him; an adventure with Him as our guide.

Effective youth workers understand that life can be the greatest adventure if we have the right guide. Their goal is to introduce youth to the guide and get them excited about the adventure of the faith journey. If we are going to see life as an adventure, we must be willing to take risks; we must be willing to try new things; experiences we are unfamiliar with; with people who force us to grow. We need to be willing to risk getting out of our comfort zones. For me, it meant going to Eastern Europe right after the revolution.

Ministry on the Orient Express

Twenty-one youth workers from the United States descended on Eastern Europe with the idea of training youth workers in the basic principles of youth ministry. To pull this off, we all had to travel on the infamous Orient Express. I hadn't even been on the train and I was spooked. The train from Vienna was sleek, modern, and aluminum. The ride was pleasant, went quickly, and emanated Austrian efficiency and vanity. "This Eastern Europe stuff ain't so bad," I thought as I waited on the platform. Then, clanging and creaking caught my eye, and I noticed a brown, wood crate on wheels. It looked like a box car with windows. People were peering expressionless out the grimy windows. As they stepped down, I noticed that they were uniformly dressed in black, brown, or gray. It looked like a scene from *Raiders of the Lost Ark*. You know, the bar scene when all kinds of unique creatures come limping through the mist.

We decided to check our baggage and rendezvous with our contact at the hotel. We finally found the baggage storage under a sign that looked like "HCJOCL#@•SO" or something like that. I felt that Hungary needed to buy more vowels from Vanna White. It's scary checking everything you own into a room the size of a gym locker only to see greasy guys laying on suitcases and smoking funny-looking cigarettes.

Five of us squashed into a taxi the size of a Yugo and we sped off to the hotel. Traffic was horrendous, but this didn't bother the cabby, he simply swerved onto the cable car track, passed all the cars, and played chicken with the cable car. To avoid certain death he veered back into traffic and screeched to a skidding stop in the middle of an intersection, against the light! I had been in Eastern Europe only minutes, and my life was flashing before me. "Why was I here?" "Why didn't I stay in sunny southern California?" Then I remembered that we were here on a mission. Yeah, that's it, "a mission from God." Well, at least *for* God. We wanted to encourage and train the youth workers in Eastern Europe. For years, they had to do everything in secret. Now, they had a little more freedom, and we wanted to act in this window of opportunity.

At the hotel we enjoyed a delicious meal and talked about why we were there. Believers from Romania, Hungary, Czechoslovakia, and Poland had asked Western missionaries to send youth workers to train their people. Reach Out Ministries, under the direction of Barry St. Clair, was asked to coordinate this trip. Our contact would be there, a full-time missionary to the East, John Howard. As we sat and stuffed ourselves, we each wondered what our trip would be like. After this meal we would separate as teams and head off to our destinations. "Would we get lost?" "Would we be able to find our contact?" "Will the KGB or Securitate trail us?" "Should we be using the 'Cone of Silence' as we talk?" Excitement, fear, and wonder filled the air.

At 1 A.M. we pulled ourselves off the cold cement floor of the cavernous train station and walked past hundreds of fellow travelers and homeless people sleeping in mounds of humanity and meager possessions. We walked carefully to avoid the pools of slush and urine. The Orient Express waited for us, belching toxic smoke and quivering in the freezing December night. We boarded the train and squeezed down the smoke-filled, twenty-four inch wide hallway, bumping virtually every person crammed into standing room only positions. I maneuvered my way to my berth and quickly fell asleep. A few hours later I was shaken by the lurching of the Orient Express; it was screeching to a halt. The conductor shouted the name of the stop, and Barry and his team were preparing to unload their baggage onto the platform of this obscure Romanian railroad depot. The conductor warned them that the train only stopped for a few minutes, and they would have to hurry. I poked my head out the window to say goodbye, I was too cozy in my berth to leave it. As I stuck my head out the window I saw a picture of speed, agility, and grace destruct into a horror movie of confusion, clumsiness, and sheer terror. Barry and his team had deftly unloaded all their stuff, only to realize it was the wrong station! As the train began to huff and puff it's way, they were throwing baggage back into the train as it pulled away.

Barry St. Clair's signature outfit is a warmup suit, and he was wearing one that day as he chased a train on the snowy plains of rural Romania. It looked like one of those movie scenes where the hero is chasing the train and leaps to catch it. That's exactly what Barry did, clutching his backpack, he dove for the train, only to fall flat on his face on the platform. A look of disgust, failure, and fear filled his face. They had managed to get most of their baggage on the train, and one of their team members. The problem was, three of the team members were stranded at the wrong depot, and none of them spoke Romanian. We hailed the conductor and he told us that the next stop was the right one, but he warned us about the gypsies who attack people and steal their possessions. I'll never forget the next stop. We left Mike alone, sitting on twelve bags of valuable stuff, at 5:30 A.M. in the cold Romanian morning. As we pulled out, I noticed a large gang of gypsies staring at Mike and laughing. I thought, "So this is what it means to be a martyr."

This was the kind of thing that filled our adventure. But in each case, God was gracious and rescued us from peril. In this case, Barry's team was soon reunited and Mike spent the morning chatting with gypsies, telling them about God, and why he'd come to Romania. They couldn't figure out why he'd brought so much stuff.

Brasov, Romania

We arrived at the Brasov depot, unloaded our luggage and tried to maintain a low profile until our contact arrived. Three youth workers trying to blend in with Romanian travelers is like Michael Jackson trying to blend in at a Shriners' Convention. It just doesn't work! We were wearing dark clothes, the right shoes, and not talking, but dozens of people stared at us. I felt I was wearing a neon sign flashing, "Secret Police—Look Here! An American!"

A woman spotted us and immediately came over and asked in broken English, "You are Americans, no?"

"Yes, we are," I said hesitantly, wanting to make sure she wasn't Securitate.

"You are here to help young people, yes?"

"Yes, we are," answered Jamie in his Tennessee accent.

"You know Shohn Hovard, yes?" she tested us with the code.

"Yes, we are with Reach Out Ministries," answered Bruce.

We introduced ourselves to this young woman, Dori, who then said, "We go now!"

I responded, "If you'd like to take us to the hotel, that would be fine."

"No, no, you stay with us," Dori replied.

"No, really, we don't want to be a burden to you," explained Bruce.

"Bruce Lee!" exclaimed Dori (she had seen the movies). "In Brasov I am boss!"

Dori's sense of humor and brashness were a welcome surprise on this venture. We had encountered one strong woman. You have to be strong to be in youth ministry, especially in Romania.

Adam, Dori's husband, returned from his job at the factory and we prepared for the training of youth workers at his church. Adam had organized a covert network of youth workers that had successfully pulled together twenty-four youth workers and hundreds of youth. To avoid detection by the Securitate, they would have their rallies in the forest, coming from different directions, at different times to avoid arousing suspicion. Our training session would be the first time youth workers met openly in a church to discuss youth ministry in over forty years!

Youth workers came from all over Transylvania to attend this training. They were nervous, because this was so new, and excited because we all sensed the beginning of something bigger than all of us.

"It is a blessing from God to see all of us in one room. Never before has this happened." said Cornel, the youth worker from the Pentecostal church.

"I never dreamed I'd see the day when we would fellowship openly with other youth workers, let alone our brothers from the west," said Emil with moist eyes.

Romania is an entire country off-balance, uncertain, confused, and tense. The church as an organization reflected this insecurity. But as individual's, most Romanian believers think deeper, pray with more sincerity, live more sacrificially, evaluate consistency, and laugh more boisterously than Westerners. They live valued lives. They understand the risk of the faith journey.

That night we had sixty-seven students come to the Explosia Bucureia (Joy Explosion), with five of them accepting Christ as their Savior and Liberator. The youth workers were elated; not only had they received training in evangelism and discipleship, but revival was breaking out in Brasov, a city previously known for its recent revolutionary martyrs. "We now can celebrate the blood of Christ in Brasov, not simply the blood of brothers and sisters!" exclaimed Daniel, the youth worker from Second Baptist Church.

The night before we left Brasov, we exchanged gifts with our hosts. Dori handed a wrapped gift to me, smiling sheepishly. Inside I found a beautiful hand-woven sweater with artistic patterns native to that area of Romania. "It's for Brooke, your little daughter," Dori said. I was astonished. Dori had followed me around the store that day, noting what sweaters I liked, and secretly purchased one for Brooke. The emotion of the moment was overwhelming. Her generosity was compelling. The sweater was expensive by Romanian standards—about four days wages! I was reminded of 2 Corinthians 8:2-4:

> Out of the most severe trial their overflowing joy and their extreme poverty welled up in rich generosity. For I testify that they gave as much as they were able, and even beyond their ability. Entirely on their own they urgently pleaded with us for the privilege of sharing in this service to the saints.

It was that winter in Romania that I learned about the reality and depth of the abundant life.

> The thief comes only to steal and kill and destroy; I have come that they may have life, and have it to the full (John 10:10).

My Romanian friends evidenced a rare, internal strength and vitality.

Principle-centered people savor life. Because their security comes from within instead of from without, they have no need to categorize and stereotype everything and everybody in life to give them a sense of certainty and predictability. They see old faces freshly, old scenes as if for the first time. They are like courageous explorers going on an expedition into uncharted territories; they are really not sure what is going to happen, but they are confident it will be exciting and growth-producing and that they will discover new territory and make new contributions. Their security lies in their initiative, resourcefulness, creativity, willpower, courage, stamina, and native intelligence rather than in the safety, protection, and abundance of their home camps, of their comfort zones.

They rediscover people each time they meet them. They are interested in them. They ask questions and get involved. They are completely present when they listen. They learn from people. They don't label them from past successes or failures. They see no one bigger than life. They are not overawed by top government figures or celebrities. They resist becoming any person's disciple. They are basically unflappable and capable of adapting virtually to anything that comes along. One of their fixed principles is flexibility. They truly lead the abundant life.[1]

My Romanian friends had seen the ravages of the thief who sought to destroy them; but they were more alive, and more committed to living a life on the cutting edge. They understood the principle that to live a life of faith means to takes risks. It means doing the right thing and living with the consequences. Faith is trusting God more than our own personal protective skills.

I came back from Romania a changed man. I began to see that I needed to challenge my youth group in the Big Adventure. I wanted them to capture the excitement of what God is doing throughout the world. There is much to be enthusiastic about. I was sharing my adventure with a group and someone in the back said, "How can you be positive about what's going on? Aren't things getting worse over there and in the world all over?"

"Yes," I replied, "some things are getting worse. The kingdom of darkness is growing, but so is the kingdom of light! And I'm rejoicing because I know which kingdom wins in the end!"

Rivers or Reservoirs?

Christ has given us His living water; we can choose to soak it up, like a giant sponge, and keep it to ourselves—a reservoir. Or we can choose to be a channel of God's benefits to others—a river. Everyday we make choices, large and small, that reveal which we are becoming—a river or a reservoir. Rivers are mighty and powerful and people are captivated by their grandeur. Reservoirs are forgettable and boring; they are too self-serving. Youth groups (like youth workers) can be either.

Churches that give away blessings are much more likely to be blessed. They are focused on others rather than themselves, open to outsiders with their new ideas and ways, inclusive rather than exclusive, outreaching rather than self-fortifying, an army of life-savers rather than a club of those once saved. These churches are for the twenty-first century. There is a basic principle for church growth: "For a church to grow, it must want to grow and be willing to pay the price." The price is least counted in dollars. It comes in the more costly currency of change. It is doing church in new ways, incorporating new people, moving out of comfort zones, and existing for others rather than for self.[2]

Effective youth workers understand the adventure of seeing needs and taking the risk of meeting them. They know they probably won't be able to meet all the needs, but they will meet some. People may even criticize them for seeking to be relevant, but they are more concerned with reaching thirsty people with the Gospel than listening to the complaints of those soaking in the Gospel.

I don't understand it, but some believers exhibit a scarcity paradigm when it comes to reaching out. They act like "we need to keep this good thing to ourselves, don't let too many people in on it!" I can't find anything further from Christ's command (Matthew 28:19-20). Mature believers see life from an abundance paradigm—they see that there is plenty of grace to go around. It's good news for the whole world! Their goal is to help as many people as they can understand that Jesus comes to offer life at its maximum potential. They are enthusiastic because they see life as an adventure that God empowers them to pursue.

How do you view life? There are three ways to walk through life:

1. Are you a **traveler**—one who just wants to get through with the trip and get to his destination? Are you simply enduring this life, until you get to heaven?

2. Are you a **tourist**—one who stops by the side of the road when he sees a "Scenic View" sign, pulls out a camera, and snaps a shot of the scenery?

3. Or are you an **explorer**—one who veers off the road most traveled and pursues adventure and the scenic places by hiking to them? We can make our life journey an adventure if we begin to see ourselves as explorers—people who dare to get outside the comfort of our car or easy chair. The effective youth worker in the future won't be appealing to tradition or comfort, but to community and the common cause of living out the big adventure.

Discussion Questions

1. Have you ever gone on an adventure that has changed your life?
   Describe what happened.

2. Why do you think the Romanian believers think deeper, pray with
   more sincerity, live more sacrificially, evaluate consistently, and laugh
   more boisterously than Westerners?

3. What do you think Jesus meant when He said, "I have come that they
   may have life and have it to the fullest."?

4. Who has been a "river" of living water in your life? What is it about
   them that makes them distinctive?

5. What do you think about the three ways to journey through life? (page
   105) Do you identify with the traveler, the tourist, or the explorer?

6. Brainstorm some ways you can become more of an explorer.

NOTES

1   Stephen R. Covey, *Principle-centered Leadership* (New York: Fireside Books, Simon Schuster Inc., 1992), 37.

2   Leith Anderson, *A Church for the 21st Century* (Minneapolis, MN: Bethany House Publishers, 1992), 192.

The Dream Team

Habit #7—"Effective Youth Workers Are Team Players and Synergistic"

I was headed to the High Sierras on a backpacking trip with a group of guys from my youth group. After six hours of driving, I was fatigued and couldn't alertly drive. We had been delayed by a horrendous traffic jam in L.A., and I was exhausted. "I'll be glad to drive," offered Steve. I was reluctant to let him drive, but he was eighteen and insured.

"Okay," I quickly conceded. "But wake me up if you have any problems."

"Okay, how do I get to Mammoth?" asked Steve.

"Just stay on this freeway until you get to 395 and take it north," I explained. I crawled in the back of the van and swiftly went to sleep.

I was awakened by the silence—no one was talking, they were all sleeping, except Steve who was drumming his fingers on the steering wheel to the beat blasting from the stereo. I glanced at the speedometer under his pulsating digit. Eighty mph! Steve was speeding! Then I noticed something that brought a fusion of anger and worry: A huge glow of light was just ahead on the freeway. Less than a few miles straight ahead was a gigantic bubble of light interrupting the navy-blue blankness of the desert night.

"Vegas!" I yelled at Steve, "You're driving us at 80 mph to Las Vegas!" My screaming woke up the other campers.

"Wow, were going to Vegas—cool!" mumbled Robert.

"You were supposed to turn on 395!" I lectured.

"I never saw it. This way's fine; we'll just find a way to go from here," explained Steve.

"Ah, it's too far from here—we're way out of the way," I whined.

"You can't get there from here," joked Lance.

"We'll have to go through Death Valley, it'll take us all night," I whimpered.

"Yeah, but look what great progress we're making. I've been going eighty to ninty mph for over two hours. Who cares if we're lost—we're making good time!" exclaimed Steve with a totally straight face.

To this day, I reflect on this episode illustrating classic ineffectiveness. "Who cares if we're doing the wrong thing? We're doing it right, aren't we?" Another analogy deals with climbing the ladder to success and reaching the top rung, only to find it leaning against the wrong building.

If we are going to be effective leaders, we need to have a broader focus than methods or efficiency. As Peter Drucker says, "Efficiency is doing things right. Effectiveness is doing the right things." One of the right things is building a team.

A strategic leader can provide direction and vision, motivate through love, and build a complementary team based on mutual respect if he is more effectiveness-minded than efficiency-minded, more concerned with direction and results than with methods, systems, and procedures.[1]

We were making good time on that freeway, but it was in the wrong direction. Sometimes we evaluate our progress in youth work by how far we've come, but we need to make sure we've gone in the right direction.

A Vacuum of Leadership

In his book, *Principle-Centered Leadership,* Stephen Covey introduces three roles that are common in all organizations:[2]

- Producer

- Manager

- Leader

Each of these roles is important to the success of the organization, but each is distinct and different. Producers are the ones who develop new ideas and products. Managers coordinate the work and the workers. Leaders set the vision and direction for the team. Without the leader, people "perish" because there is no vision. Strategic leadership is crucial for the continual success of any team.

Leadership deals with direction—with making sure that the ladder is leaning against the right wall. Management deals with speed. To double one's speed in the wrong direction, however, is the very definition of foolishness. Leadership deals with vision—with keeping the mission in sight—and with effectiveness and results. Management deals with establishing structure and systems to get those results. It focuses on efficiency, cost-benefit analyses, logistics, methods, procedures, and policies. Leadership focuses on the top line. Management focuses on the bottom line. Leadership derives its power from values and correct principles. Management organizes resources to serve selected objectives to produce the bottom line.[3]

Effective leaders are team builders. They acknowledge that to perform at peak levels requires the cooperation and contribution of each teammate. The challenge is to minimize the distraction and the tension on the team. Individual differences can be affirmed—we each have our strengths and our roles to play. Mutual appreciation and respect creates an environment for a competent and complementary team—one where the strength lies in differences.

> The body is a unit, though it is made up of many parts; and though all its parts are many, they form one body. So it is with Christ. . . . If the whole body were an eye, where would the sense of hearing be? If the whole body were an ear, where would the sense of smell be? But in fact God has arranged the parts in the body, every one of them, just as He wanted them to be. If they were all one part, where would the body be? As it is, there are many parts, but one body (1 Corinthians 12:12, 17-20).

Each part of the Body of Christ is meaningful and offers something beneficial to the whole. It would be a disservice to the Body to try to make each part function the same. It would be ineffective and devalue the individuality and giftedness of each part.

The same is true with effective teams of youth workers—each person needs to be valued for their individual worth and contribution. Their "differentness" needs to be celebrated rather than minimized. The goal is to make each strength more productive and each weakness more irrelevant. The focus is on contribution, affirmation, and appreciation.

This kind of thinking requires a paradigm shift. It would involve at least these five changes:

TEAM BUILDER ⟶ PARADIGM SHIFT

1. From: *Program to People*

Our paradigm should shift from the needs of our program to the needs of the people. If we are going to build an effective team, we need to be concerned with the needs of our team players as well as the needs of our targeted ministry people. This has implications for how we recruit people for positions on our youth worker team. If we switch our paradigm from program to people, we won't recruit someone into a position they aren't gifted in or called to. In other words, we won't manipulate a person to fill a position.

2.   From: *Production to Principles*

Instead of pursuing the production of a program, our new paradigm will be interested in principle-driven ministry. We've discussed in earlier chapters that it's easier to build a team around the concept of building principles into people's lives rather than simply building toward a production. People sometimes feel used when all they did was contribute to something flashy, but short-lived. In contrast, people feel valued when they experience personal growth as they make a commitment with others to a cause. Production and principle sometimes look a lot alike. The difference is that production looks for the short-term payoff, and principle-oriented ministry focuses on long-term growth.

3.   From: *Past to Future*

Team building requires a future-focused perspective. We can't afford the luxury of looking at life through the rearview mirror. People are interested in joining a team that has a future, and not simply a "blast from the past!"

One of the saddest interviews I've had was with a historic church with a rich evangelical tradition. They showed me pictures of their historic church in its heyday. They dropped the names from the "Who's Who" of the church's past. Then they asked me if I wanted to "join their team." I felt like I was being recruited to live in a mausoleum! All the heroes were dead, the staff lived in their shadows, and there was no vision for the future. It's difficult to be motivated to join a team which has a past, but no future. I turned the job down. I'd rather sign on with a team that has a promising future than a notable past. People are more committed to shaping the future than preserving the past.

4.   From: *Obstacles to Opportunities*

People love to be around winners, they crowd the winner's locker room after the big game. But the loser's locker room is quiet and reflective. In the game of life we see people who always seem like winners—even in the midst of adversity. Their secret? Turn every obstacle into an opportunity. Turn every failure into a lesson. If we have a team with this paradigm, even if we are technically mediocre, we will have a decided advantage. Why? Because this positive, what-can-we-learn-from-this mentality keeps people in an open and learning mentality. They remain open to new input. People who are teachable are more capable because they are open to receive additional input which will help them transform every obstacle into an opportunity.

5. From: *Fear of Criticism to Cultural Relevance*

People operate from either a motivation of fear or desire. Both are very strong motivators. In building an effective team, it is important to minimize fear as a motive and emphasize desire. If we are to bring out the best of each team member, we need to address their fears, accept and affirm them as valid, and then gently point them towards the fears and needs of others. I am not saying, "Forget about your fears; other people have it worse." I am saying, people sense a degree of control and courage when they realize they are not alone with their fears and are able to understand and support others. When we share our fears with each other we gain courage from each other. A team must be willing to have a foundation based in reality. We must be willing to look at each other and say, "I'm afraid this might not work," and feel supported.

I am convinced that many ministries are destined to ineffectiveness because they are motivated by fear. Think about how many times you have heard there was a need in your community and someone had a creative idea on how to meet that need, but it was quenched by a comment like, "That's a great idea, but it would really raise questions from some of the deacons." Or, "That might work in another place, but here it would be seen as worldly, or compromising." In the guise of being spiritual and sensitive ("politically correct") leaders often make decisions out of fear.

Jesus focused on meeting needs regardless of the social fallout. In an awkward moment at dinner, an uninvited female with a dubious reputation crashed the party and with great passion kissed Christ's feet. As her tears dribbled, she wiped His feet with her long, flowing hair. The religious big shots of the day commented on Jesus' lack of discernment and discretion.

> If this man were a prophet, He would know who is touching Him and what kind of woman she is—that she is a sinner (Luke 7:39).

Christ didn't respond to this criticism, instead, he ignored the Pharisees and utilized the teachable moment to tell Simon Peter a story about forgiveness. This is the paradigm to have: always remembering that we have been forgiven much and we should not be critical of others, but see them as fellow sinners in need of grace. The other side of this parable is not allowing critical religious people to keep us from meeting the needs of secular folks.

Christ models for us how to be culturally relevant without compromise. He was socializing with sinners—those who pretended they weren't and those who knew they were. He was available to people who needed the Gospel. He was on their turf and was relaxed—they were having dinner. His focus was on the needs of people, not His need to look socially respectful. In this case, I think He walked the balance by showing respect for the woman's need, but also by showing respect to the need of the religious elite. By allowing the woman to continue anointing His feet, Christ was able to set up a situation which would illustrate to the cynical saints their need of true repentance. Christ affirmed both needs for spiritual renewal by being relevant to the sinful woman and the sinful Pharisees. In the midst of all this dramatic tension, Christ did not compromise the Gospel. The focus was consistently on sin, forgiveness, and love. There is talk today that being culturally relevant is an automatic compromise of the Gospel. In this case, Christ shows us that we can be culturally relevant without being ashamed of the Gospel.

A Strategy for Synergy

Once we have the paradigm for team building, we need to have a strategy for synergy. Synergy is the state in which the whole is more important than the sum of the parts. Synergistic youth work seeks to affirm the value and contribution of each individual to the team. The youth worker who understands synergy will be able to make students and staff feel valuable by affirming their personal contribution and uniqueness. She will also be able to show individuals how their contribution and giftedness benefits the whole group. As each person feels valued, affirmed and meaningful, a spirit of teamwork begins to develop. Synergy can't be forced; it must be grown. As it grows, it takes on a life of its own. This life is energy produced by the cooperative spirit of people effectively working together.

Effective influencing and understanding spring largely from healthy relationships among the members of the group. Leaders need to foster environments and work processes within which people can develop high-quality relationships in the group with which we work.[4]

From a biblical perspective, synergy begins with an understanding of the diversity of spiritual gifts and God-given personalities. As we understand and respect our diversity we are able to begin trusting each other and learning to value each other. We learn to think in a new way about the strengths of others. We realize that we can sing in a key we don't usually sing, and still sound harmonious. Effective leaders are learners because they are always open to a new way of doing things—not simply their way. They seek to empower people to make decisions on their own, and determine their own sphere of influence.

For example, we assigned our students to small group leaders who made their own choices of what they will do with their small group. There are basic guidelines to work within, but there is a lot of freedom for the leaders to choose. With their student's input, they decide on outside activities that they want to do as a small group, how to structure their group time, and the level of accountability and care they want to have as a group. This emphasis on decentralized empowerment and grass-roots decision-making is not simply a trend in business, it is a principle that is centuries old.

> There are different kinds of gifts, but the same Spirit. There are different kinds of service, but the same Lord. There are different kinds of working, but the same God works all of them in all men. . . . The body is a unit, though it is made up of many parts; and though all its parts are many, they form one body. So it is with Christ. For we were all baptized by one Spirit into one body—whether Jews or Greeks, slave or free—and we were all given the one Spirit to drink (1 Corinthians 12:4-6, 12-14).

Effective youth workers understand synergy and work to develop it. They know a team with synergy will recruit for itself because prospective volunteers will want to get in on the action. People are seeking the meaning, encouragement, and community that they can experience on a spiritually unified team.

The leader who can learn the laws of group morale becomes a highly valuable commodity, for not only does good esprit de corps enable people to get the job done in half the time, it also draws in new people. Some of the most successful churches, for instance, are led by pastors who do not have magnetic personalities. Their success is due rather to the skill with which they build an enthusiastic, cohesive congregation. So in such cases people are drawn not so much to the leader but to the group feeling—the high-energy atmosphere. Good leaders set out to do far more than build allegiance to themselves, which is important, of course, but it is not enough. It is also necessary to build into the organization an allegiance to each other.[5]

Enemies of Team Spirit

One of the quickest synergy-killers is **competition**. It can bring out the worst in a team if members are competing against each other instead of their common opponent. As Christians, our enemy is Satan. We need to stand together against him and all that would seek to elevate him and destroy Christian faith. Our primary competition is in the spiritual arena.

A healthy dose of competition in the social arena can be helpful. An active game of volleyball, a competition between classes to raise money for missions, a friendly softball game against another church youth group, and recreation involving parents against kids can be very effective in creating a team spirit.

Competition destroys synergy when the focus becomes winning. I know of a youth director who organized volleyball games on Sunday afternoons, but few of his youth would attend. He had to be on the winning team; if he wasn't, he'd fume and fuss and stomp off to his office for a pity party. His competitive spirit killed any opportunity for community in that youth group. There will always be competition in athletics, business, and life. What must change is the intensity that turns competition into combat. A wise youth worker knows how to tame competition with cooperation.

A look at the root meaning of "compete" is revealing—even surprising. The Latin source is "competere," meaning "to come together, agree, be suitable, belong, compete for." Nothing in this original definition of competing suggests the need for a killer instinct. We have added that little feature by coming to believe that excellence can be achieved only at the expense of others.[6]

Many of us are getting fed up with the win-lose, self-centered, look-out-for-number-one "me-ism" that is common in our culture. There has got to be a way we can cooperate, even in the midst of some lively competition.

If you have a team member who is being competitive and concerned about himself winning, and hurting the team in the process, share with him these ideas on competition. Let him know that his killer instinct is from the world and not from the Spirit of God. Challenge him to fight the fight that is worth fighting. The competitive spirit is good, but sometimes it gets misdirected.

> For our struggle is not against flesh and blood, but against the rulers, against the authorities, against the powers of this dark world and against the spiritual forces of evil in the heavenly realms (Ephesians 6:12).

Another enemy of team spirit is a **lack of communication**. Everyone on the team should be able to describe in a sentence what is the purpose of your youth ministry. These descriptions should sound amazingly alike because you have worked on communicating purpose. Once you have developed and articulated your purpose statement, come up with three or four priorities for your youth ministry. For instance:

1. To develop small groups where every student is assigned to a leader for weekly care and Bible study.
2. To offer events that appeal to pre-Christians as well as Christians.
3. To challenge our youth to practice their faith by offering service projects four times a year.

If a youth leader is asked what the group is all about, he can share the purpose statement (in his own words) and say, "We are working to have each kid in a small group. Make it a safe place for him to invite his friends from school, and challenge him to live out his faith by serving." This type of common language significantly helps establish community and enhances communication. Communication is key to team spirit.

Communicate extensively to create the link between causes and the commitment individual employees make to those causes. You can't force people to be committed; neither can you control whether they stay committed. The best approach is to be the source of clear, consistent, honest information. **When in doubt, tell people too much**. The more they know about your cause, the more they can help in ways you wouldn't have expected. The more they find they can help, the more commitment they feel. Respect people enough to be straight with them about the down side as well as the up side; that too, strengthens commitment.[7] (emphasis added)

A third enemy of team spirit is **conflict**. There will come a time when team members disagree. Your role as leader is not to ignore it, though, in some cases this will work; seek to resolve the conflict. Separate the people from the problem. Extract the personalities and focus on the issue. If people feel they have been heard, they usually choose to move toward a reconciliation or compromise. It is important to seek first to understand rather than be understood when resolving conflict. Make sure you do much listening and little lecturing. An effective team leader tries hard not to lose anyone over a disagreement, but also never allows conflict to destroy the team.

Affirm both sides that conflict is natural and a part of being on a team. It doesn't have to be disastrous as long as we talk about it and play fair. Some of our best lessons can come out of times of conflict. Encourage people to talk directly to the persons they are having trouble with, and not talk to others unnecessarily. If you have one of these troublemakers who consistently seeks conflict, share with him the following verse.

"He who loves a quarrel loves sin" (Proverbs 17:19).

Putting Together the Dream Team

The kind of people you choose will determine how much synergy you have on your team. Certain qualities make it easier to pull together a team. I like the characteristics listed by Jim Marian in his book, *Growing Up Christian*.[8] Jim reminds us of the importance of relationship with youth as we seek to disciple them. Three traits that characterize a relational approach to discipling youth are:

1. Availability

We are so busy today that youth have few adults to relate to. Being available is a way we can show teens that they are important to us. Hanging out with kids helps them believe what we say because they see us putting it into action.

2. Modeling

Christian kids are often in the process of throwing away the style of their parents' faith and are in search for a faith style that fits them. Providing alternative models for a healthy faith is one important role for a youth worker. I seek to recruit staff who look different, act different, like different music, and relate to kids differently than me. But they must have in common a growing, passionate love for Christ and a desire to see that develop in teens.

3. Accountability

It is my opinion that all youth workers need to be held accountable to someone. I'm not talking checking in weekly for what you ate, how often you did your quiet times, or shared your faith. I'm talking about having a mentor or small group who will hold you accountable to grow as a believer. It could be the youth team itself. Accountability helps us balance the external with the internal. We can't ask our students to be accountable if we aren't. Groups that exercise some kind of accountability amongst their leaders tend not to have as many moral catastrophes as groups that don't. I've had youth leaders share that their marriage was in trouble. The team kept this confidence and prayed for this couple. One of the staff offered to pay for marital counseling, another couple invited the couple (at their expense) to go with them to a marriage renewal weekend. A year later, the troubled couple said, "If it wasn't for the accountability and care from this team, we would be divorced today! We feel loved and cared for by you. Thanks."

Now that's a team worth being on!

The Effective Team Leader:

1. Has vision
2. Has character and integrity
3. Searches out competence
4. Leads through serving
5. Communicates easily at all levels
6. Is approachable and available to his/her followers (is a listener)
7. Is open to contrary opinion
8. Is committed to fairness and advocates it
9. Values the contributions, skills, and talents of others, but values the person more than the task
10. Makes it a priority to be in touch with the organization and its work
11. Is a spokesperson and diplomat
12. Is able to see the big picture (beyond his/her own area of focus)
13. Understands and passes on the stories and culture of the organization
14. Tells *WHY* rather than *HOW*
15. Can rejoice with those who rejoice and weep with those who weep
16. Is able to utilize different styles of leadership in different settings/situations
17. Is committed to a legacy (something that lives beyond him/her)
18. Is accountable and holds his followers to accountability
19. Enables his/her followers to realize their full potential as persons
20. Has earned the respect of his/her followers

Discussion Questions

1. Have you ever had the experience of making progress but in the wrong direction? Compare stories.

2. This book is on being effective. How does that contrast with being efficient?

3. How does leadership differ from management?

4. How do we reconcile individuality with a sense of team?

5. How do the following five paradigm shifts help promote team spirit and synergy from:
   - Program to people

   - Production to principles

   - Past to future

   - Obstacles to opportunities

   - Fear of criticism to cultural relevance

6. Study the 20 qualities of "The Effective Team Leader" on page 119. Pick three you are currently using, and three you'd like to see developed this year. Discuss with your group ways you can grow in these three areas, while maintaining your current qualities.

NOTES

1   Stephen R. Covey, *Principle-Centered Leadership* (New York: Fireside Books, Simon & Schuster Inc., 1991), 249.

2   Ibid., 244.

3   Ibid., 246.

4   Max Depree, *Leadership Is an Art* (New York: Bantam Doubleday Dell Publishing Group, Inc., 1989), 25.

5   Alan Loy Mc Ginnis, *Bringing Out the Best in People* (Minneapolis, MN: Augsburg Publishing House, 1985), 136-37.

6   Denis Waitley, *The Double Win* (Old Tappan, NJ: Fleming H. Revell Company, 1985), 202.

7   Robert Waterman, *The Renewal Factor* (New York: Bantam Doubleday Dell Publishing Group, Inc., 1987), 336.

8   Jim Marian, *Growing Up Christian* (Wheaton, IL: Victor Books, 1992), 112-14.

In Search of Sabbath

Habit #8—"Effective Youth Workers
Are Committed to Personal Renewal"

The house was silent as I pulled my dinner out of the microwave oven. I was famished. It was 10 P.M. Sunday and I was sitting down with my nuked potato. It had been a full day—teaching, interacting, leading meetings, and speaking at our high school meeting. I felt like all I had been doing was talking and giving all day. I was totally drained, on empty and irritable. I was glad that Suzanne, my wife, had gone to bed—it probably saved an argument.

As I stared out the front window, I realized I was in trouble—I couldn't keep up at this pace and expect my life, marriage, and ministry to hold together. As a father I was beginning to understand the need to model balance to my daughters and be available to them. As I took a deeper look into my soul, I wasn't pleased. Underneath the facade of church chat and holy hype was a heart that was cynical, aloof, and cold towards God. It hadn't happened overnight—it had been a process of drifting—kind of like a marriage that passively becomes alienated due to neglect. God was a stranger to me, although I referred to Him often. Of course, that was on a professional basis, not a personal basis. The danger of full-time youth work is that it becomes a job, not a journey. The spiritual discovery gets traded in for a religious diversion regimen.

As I scraped the last piece of cheddar cheese from the paper plate, I searched the recesses of my empty spirit. How I longed for the days when my heart was passionate for the things of God. *How had I lost it? Couldn't I see the loss?* It was that brisk winter night I told God, and myself, that I was going to do something about the cold barrenness of my soul.

My pursuit to rekindle my passion for God led me to discover a key principle about spiritual renewal: "Effective ministry starts from the inside out." Ministry is more passion than profession. Ministry is as much who we are as what we do. In all that goes on in youth ministry, spiritual energy is always required. I had been living and working as if this premise wasn't true. I was counting on my determination and my energy level to get me through. I hadn't recharged my own soul, and I was trying to minister out of my emptiness.

The supply of the energy, or passion, within the inner spirit is not inexhaustible; it can and will be depleted. Young men and women tend not to know that. They surmise that the brute strength of their physical energy level can carry them on indefinitely. It can work for a while, but not forever! One day, having ignored this possibility, they awake to the extreme inner stress of exhaustion of spirit. It is a terribly confusing experience.[1]

I was perplexed because I thought if I served God by doing all this youth work, He would recharge me spiritually and keep me plugged into His providential power pack. I was disappointed with God because I was working so hard for Him, and He didn't seem to appreciate it. I was irritated with God because He had given me all of the ministry responsibility, but had not given me the perseverance and strength to pull it off.

As I took a harder look, I saw the confusion, the disappointment, the anger and the blaming—and I realized I was drained. I had seen this before in myself—usually after a successful camp, or some great spiritual victory in the youth group. The desert depression followed the mountain top celebration. I am learning it's not God's responsibility to keep me charged up spiritually—it's mine. For years I thought God wanted my work, it turns out He wants me! He can get His work done with or without me, but He desires intimacy with me. Ministry is designed to drive us to God, not away from Him. Ministry is challenging and draining because God wants us to depend on Him for our renewal and strength.

It's so easy to let the demands of youth work crowd in and leave no time for spiritual renewal. We want to do well, we want to be considered "successful," so we run harder and longer to get the job done. But it's a subtle distraction from the real thing.

When worldly success dominates our thinking, we focus our attention on power. We try to orchestrate situations to put ourselves in the best light, rather than simply serving and leaving our reputations in God's hands. The temptation to be successful is the third temptation of Jesus. After showing Jesus all the kingdoms of the world and their splendor, the devil said, "All this I will give You if You will bow down and worship me" (Matthew 4:9). "Circumvent God's way, sacrifice your priorities, and I will give you success beyond belief," says the devil—to Jesus and to us.[2]

There are no shortcuts to spiritual vitality. Spiritual life is an organic relationship which takes time—you have to grow it; it can't be rushed. Take a good look at any voice promising shortcuts to spiritual success; it may be the voice of the deceiver. Spiritual growth needs to be seen with a long-term perspective. Personal renewal is not some quick fix, but a lifelong process. It is not manipulation of the variables, but a walk behind the Good Shepherd. True spirituality isn't simply how we behave, in fact, it has more to do with *being* than behavior. Renewal of the soul can't be quantified, it is a qualitative experience that is difficult to describe, let alone measure. Teilhard de Chardin said, "We are not human beings having a spiritual experience. We are spiritual beings having a human experience." The challenge is getting back to the spiritual priority.

I have discovered that "private defeats follow public victories." I am most depressed, or drained following a momentous occasion in the youth group. I find myself feeling alone and defeated. I'm not sure how much is emotional and how much is spiritual—but I feel down. I'm sure much of it is physical fatigue as well. I used to take Monday off and stumble through the day trying to recover from my Sunday ordeal. Then I realized I was giving myself and my family my worst day. I decided to switch my day off to Friday (Thursday, if we have youth activities), and instantly I discovered energy for my day off that I hadn't had in years. I now give Monday to quietly recovering by reading and doing easy tasks around the office, like catching up with my correspondence. I find that on Monday I care about people, but don't want to be with them, so I write notes to students, staff, parents, and friends. After a day of being in "recharge mode" and not taking many calls or appointments, I'm ready to face the week. Monday is a great day to be in the office if you are a youth pastor, you don't get too many calls—everyone thinks you take it off! If you are a volunteer youth worker it's important that you too carve out time in your busy schedule to recharge after intense times of ministry.

Just as I have discovered that "private defeats follow public victories," I have also found that "private victories precede public victories." If we expect to see spiritual victories in our youth group, we will need to personally experience them first.

Someone once told me, "You can't take youth beyond where you are spiritually." As I thought about this, I realized I need to be experiencing my own spiritual growth and renewal before I can expect my youth group to. I needed to have personal, private victories before I would experience public victories.

Stephen Covey in his book *Principle-Centered Leadership* presents the idea that principle-centered leaders exercise for self-renewal; it is a discipline of their daily life. This isn't simply physical exercise, but mental, emotional, and spiritual as well. These are the four disciplines of personal renewal: physical, mental, emotional, and spiritual exercises.

I'm convinced that if a person will spend one hour a day on these basic exercises, he or she will improve the quality, productivity, and satisfaction of every other hour of the day, including the depth and restfulness of sleep. No other single hour of your day will return as much as the hour you invest in sharpening the saw, that is, in exercising these four dimensions of the human personality. . . . We must never get too busy sawing to take time to sharpen the saw, never too busy driving to take time to get gas. . . . If I do this hour of exercise early in the morning, it is like a private victory and just about guarantees public victories throughout the day. But if I take the course of least resistance and neglect all or part of this program, I forfeit that private victory and find myself uprooted by public pressures and stresses throughout the day.[3]

Stephen Covey is advocating a priority of self-discipline that was modeled by Jesus.

Very early in the morning, while it was still dark, Jesus got up, left the house and went off to a solitary place, where he prayed (Mark 1:35).

Jesus faced pressure-packed days. To prepare for them He started early by spending time with His Father. In the midst of the breathless pace of bringing to life a dead girl, feeding the 5,000, and dodging the sword of King Herod, we find Jesus quietly breathing prayers to His Father. As He looked to the heavens He received the focus and the solitude that He needed for the day. Jesus was fully God/fully man, but He still needed a place for renewal. Even the Son of God needed a quiet place to recharge. Not only does Christ model this discipline, but He encourages His faithful followers to do so.

The apostles gathered around Jesus and reported to Him all they had done and taught. Then, because so many people were coming and going that they did not even have a chance to eat, He said to them, "Come with me by yourselves to a quiet place and get some rest. So they went away by themselves in a boat to a solitary place" (Mark 6:30-32).

The apostles were excited about the miracles and the "growth in the program." They focused on what they had done and taught. Jesus knew the danger of being excited, busy, and focusing on our own accomplishments. He knew it was a recipe for burn out. They had been so swamped with meeting needs and being surrounded by people that they hadn't taken the time to rest and renew. I think it's interesting to see that Jesus didn't say, "That's great guys, wow, we fed 4,000! Let's try for 5,000 today!" Christ could have pushed for performance, but He called them to rest.

That is my concern for you, dear youth worker. Do you find yourself wrapped up in "what you have done and taught"? Is your excitement in your performance or in the Person? Jesus would call you, faithful follower, "Come with Me, by yourselves, leave your calendar, your crowd breaker book, and your camp planning; let's go to a quiet place, where we can rest." Do you hear Him?

As I reflect on Christ's solitary times, I discover that these weren't times of preparation for the future, but for that day. As youth workers we often fall into the pattern of "spend time with God now because He'll use it in the future." It's really easy to imagine our dreams as God's will for our life. We think God is leading us through something because it will help us in the future. But what we see as the process, God sees as the end itself. God's purpose always involves the day at hand; He wants me to depend on Him and His power for today. Jesus pushed His disciples to get in the boat and go on ahead of Him while He went up the mountain to pray (Mark 6:45). As the storm whipped up the lake into a white-capped froth, Jesus came strolling by, walking on the water; He almost passed them when they spotted Him and cried out. In the middle of the storms of life Jesus wants us to call out to Him. He wanted to teach His disciples to see Him in spite of their fear and the pounding surf. That's His goal for each of us—to know that He can walk on the storms of my life right now.

God's training is for now, not later. His purpose is for this very minute, not for sometime in the future. We have nothing to do with what will follow our obedience, and we are wrong to concern ourselves with it. What people call preparation, God sees as the goal itself.[4]

It's easy to use our quiet times as preparation for the next youth group lesson. We may try to discipline ourselves from that and focus on our own renewal, only to be interrupted by the thought, "This would be a great teaching for my next series!"

To help myself combat this temptation, I have two study periods each week. Tuesday mornings are primarily what I call "Personal Study." I focus on growing as a person and recharging my spirit and mind. Others have called this, "Offensive Study"—a time to move out against the enemy by preparing the warrior. This would be in contrast to "Defensive Study," which is preparing to deliver tonight's Bible study. I prefer to use the terms "Personal Study" and "Teaching Study." My quiet times are in the morning, before my feet hit the carpet. I read Scripture, think about it, and then pray. These morning times are much more meaningful now that I have my study times.

My quiet times are just for me. I don't have to prepare a lesson. I prepare my life.

Without solitude it is virtually impossible to live a spiritual life. Solitude begins with a time and place for God, and Him alone.[5]

Teaching Study

My Thursday mornings are spent preparing for the teaching for the weekend. My administrative assistant holds calls for me for both of these study periods, and I don't schedule any appointments. I usually can get in all of my teaching study because I am refreshed from my personal study.

If you are a volunteer youth worker you will need to adjust this idea to fit your schedule. For example, you could have your personal quiet times in the morning and pick one week night to study for your teaching, and skip one hour of TV each week to read a good Christian book (like this one!).

If you find you are running out of time preparing for teaching, it could be that you need to spend less time. That's right, spend some of your teaching prep time on refreshing your own spirit. Chances are, a renewed mind and spirit will be able to comprehend and process spiritual truth much faster. If I cheat on my personal study, and let other things crowd in, I find it takes me twice as long to prepare my lessons.

It's like that car repair commercial, "You can pay me now, or you can pay me later." Invest on recharging your soul now, it's a lot less expensive than recovering from total burnout.

Spiritual renewal is only part of the battle for personal renewal. Sometimes we just need a break from the pressures and demands of youth work. For those of you in full-time youth work, it is important for you to have one complete day off each week. That means, not calling the office, not stopping by the church, not taking calls that deal with your work, or socializing with church people who seem like work! Ridge Burns offers four helpful rules for preserving your day off.

Rule #1—"I leave my work at the office on my day off." I don't take phone calls unless they are emergencies. . . . I totally drop out of ministry to the church and minister only to my family.

Rule #2—"I plan my day off with my family one week in advance."

Rule #3—"I try not to skip my devotions on my day off." Devotions help me think more about my family. I pray for them before they get up, and that allows me to approach my day off in a more spiritual way.

Rule #4—"I am as creative on my day off as I am in youth ministry." When I think about how carefully I plan a retreat to make sure that kids are entertained, ministered to, and challenged in their faith, I am embarrassed at how little time and creative energy I spend helping my family enjoy those same kinds of experiences.[6]

Cultivating the Garden

My wife is a "colorscape" gardener. She adds color to existing landscapes by planting flowers. She likes to amend the soil by adding nutrients and additives which will naturally aid the plants as they grow. One of her clients has a beautiful estate home with expensive landscaping and a huge lawn. But as she began working the soil in the flower garden, she realized no one had ever amended the soil or cultivated the garden. It was ironic to have this mansion of a house and have hardpan dirt in front of it. It had the potential to be in "House and Garden" magazine, but it wasn't living up to it.

The same is true of people. God has given us the potential to be beautiful gardens—masterpieces of His grace and care; but many of us are hardpan— we resist the trauma of being cultivated. If we want to experience God's renewing beauty, we must be willing to till our souls.

Gardening involves the following steps:

CULTIVATION

PLANTING

WATERING

WAITING

PROTECTING

HARVEST

Gardening our souls for harvest requires the same process. We must be willing to let God CULTIVATE our lives. That means we must let Him break through the surface and till us. A tiller turns over the top soil with the soil beneath it—it mixes the soil and adds oxygen. The soil on the surface benefits by being turned under, and the lower soil benefits by being turned up. The same is true of our lives. God seeks to turn over that which has been unmoved, we may like it left untouched, but for the harvest, it needs to be cultivated. We get so comfortable with the status quo, that we forget a little change is good for all growing things. To reject the discomfort of cultivation is to reject the promise of the harvest. Cultivation involves studying your present life and deciding what you would like to change.

PLANTING is the second step towards a growing spirit. We need to plant seeds that will increase the potential of the harvest. Maybe it would involve scheduling time for exercising the four disciplines for personal renewal— daily exercises which challenge us physically, mentally, emotionally, and spiritually. For me, I try to set goals for these disciplines. Mine are, exercise four times a week; quiet times six days a week; three evenings home per week; reading for four hours per week (instead of TV); and writing for four hours per week. I don't always make these goals, but I am increasing my harvest potential by planting seeds of renewal.

WATERING is the concept of daily adding input for renewal for my life. This may mean choosing to listen to positive, uplifting music, instead of the news. It may mean eating lunch by myself in the park and enjoying the beauty of God's creation. I water my soul by meditating on God's word and reflecting on His past faithfulness. Through prayer and positive reminders I water my soul daily.

WAITING is often overlooked, but it is an integral part of growth. Waiting gives us time to give up our agenda to discover God's. It allows us the time to develop relationships with others who will support us and share with us. When we are waiting we have time to dialogue. As we discuss, we process information and begin to expand ourselves. A relaxed, authentic conversation makes each person feel more alive and filled with more capacity than before the dialogue. This kind of growth can't be rushed. We need to learn the value of patience if we are to maximize the lessons that can only be learned in God's waiting room.

PROTECTING includes the idea of keeping ourselves safe. There are environments and people which could be destructive to us. If we are going to be harvesters we are going to have to take some precautions. We will need to evaluate all input coming into our garden, we'll have to screen for bugs and rodents. Disease is another enemy we need to be protected from. It may look like a milky dust, but some fungi can be deadly to a hybrid rose. We just can't say "yes" to everything that wants to come into our garden (lives). We need some boundaries, we'll have to say "no" to many good things so we can say "yes" to the best. The best protection for our soul/gardens is prayer. It is our sentry against the enemies of the garden.

HARVEST is the reward for those who are willing to work the gardens of their souls. It is the time, energy, creativity, and fruit of our labor. It is a prized blossom we cherish and bring glory to. In youth work, the harvest is the change in our youth. It is the observable growth, the increased joy, the application of God's truth, and the experience of renewal, or life-change. Different crops will mature at different times; the harvest comes for people in different seasons. If we follow the law of the harvest we will nurture growth and renewal, in our own souls first, then in the gardens of our youth.

Being confident of this, that He who began a good work in you will carry it on to completion until the day of Christ Jesus. It is right for me to feel this way about all of you, since I have you in my heart . . . and this is my prayer: that your love may abound more and more in knowledge and depth and insight, so that you may be able to discern what is best and may be pure and blameless until the day of Christ, filled with the fruit of righteousness that comes through Jesus Christ—to the glory of God (Philippians 1:6-7, 9-11).

I am confident that God will continue to grow within you the seeds of effectiveness. It will be by His power that these eight habits will bear His harvest—the "fruits of righteousness."

Success is reaching goals that benefit me and others. We will be effective in our youth work when we leave a legacy of contribution and impact.

> How do you measure success?
> To laugh often and much;
> To win the respect of intelligent people
> and the affection of children;
> To earn the appreciation of honest critics
> and endure the betrayal of false friends;
> To appreciate beauty;
> To find the best in others;
> To leave the world a bit better,
> whether by a healthy child, a garden patch,
> a redeemed social condition, or a job well done;
> To know even one other life has breathed easier
> because you have lived
> This is to have succeeded.
>
> *Ralph Waldo Emerson*

Discussion Questions

1. How do you feel when you are "burnt out?" How do you react and relate to others?

2. How have you experienced the maxim, "Effective ministry starts from the inside out"?

3. Describe a time when a private defeat followed a public victory.

4. What kind of environment and experience is renewing for you?

5. Review the six steps for gardening the soul. Expand and explore the definitions. Which of these sound appealing to your soul? Cultivation, planting, watering, waiting, protecting, or harvest?

6. What might be some practical actions to develop this quality of renewal in your life?

NOTES

1 Gordon MacDonald, *Restoring Your Spiritual Passion* (Nashville, TN: Oliver- Nelson Books, Thomas Nelson Publishers Inc., 1986), 40.

2 Paul Borthwick, *Feeding Your Forgotten Soul* (Grand Rapids, MI: Zondervan Publishing House, 1990), 36.

3 Stephen R. Covey, *Principle-centered Leadership* (New York: Fireside Books, Simon & Schuster Inc., 1992), 38-9.

4 Oswald Chambers, *My Utmost for His Highest* (Grand Rapids, MI: Discovery House Publishers, 1992), July 28.

5 Henri Nouwen, *Out of Solitude—Three Meditations on the Christian Life* (Notre Dame, IN: Ave Maria Press, 1984), 14.

6 Ridge Burns, *No Youth Worker Is an Island* (Wheaton, IL: Victor Books, 1992), 156.

Becoming Effective

"Implementing the Eight Habits"

Effective leaders come from a variety of backgrounds and personalities, but they tend to have common qualities that make them effective. We have explored eight qualities of the effective youth worker. We have learned that effectiveness is an internal issue, more than an external one. Who we *are* has much influence on how effective we are. *Being* impacts *doing*.

Youth workers, who are effective, don't simply know the "secrets" of youth ministry. They have developed personal habits that translate into powerful patterns. They are women and men of vision, who can implement their vision into reality.

Habits are sometimes easy to fall into, difficult to develop, and sometimes, nearly impossible to break. They can be good or bad. In this book, we have focused on developing positive habits. But, to be more effective with your new habits, you may need to be liberated from some old habits. Old patterns, perspectives, and paradigms may be keeping you from growing fresh and vital habits.

Forget the former things; do not dwell on the past. See I am doing a new thing! Now it springs up, do you not perceive it? (Isaiah 43:18-19)

Dr. Denis Waitley[1] says that habits are fragile at first and can easily be broken—like cobwebs. But in time, and with practice, they can be like cables—giving support and strength to your life. That's our goal—"from cobwebs to cables"!

If we are going to impact youth for eternity we will need internalized habits which will empower us toward effectiveness. Effective youth work is an internal issue: "For eternal impact, focus on internal growth."

We live in a culture that is rapidly becoming discouraged with the personality ethic. We are in search of quality—from the inside out. As youth workers, we are in a privileged position because we can help shape the next generation to be committed to growth in character. The best place to start is with ourselves.

I was speaking to 700 high school winter campers. I asked them to complete my sentence, "If it's worth doing, it's. . . ." To my amazement all 700 echoed in unison "worth doing well." I teased them about having the same mother and father, and asked them why they would all parrot the same line. "Have you been brain washed?" I quizzed.

Where do we get this idea that if it's "worth doing, it's worth doing well"? If something is *worth* doing, it's worth doing poorly, or with mediocrity! I asked the campers to chant after me, "If it's worth doing, it's worth doing with mediocrity." They laughed and filed it in their memory to use with their parents; but there was an immense liberty that came over that camp. Many of those students were living in families and coming from youth groups which were performance-based and perfectionistic.

If something is worth doing, *just do it!* Don't worry about the results. One of my favorite movies is "What About Bob." In it we learn a principle which would apply here: Baby Steps—taking small steps in the right direction to help us through, one day at a time.

I want you to "Baby Step" with these habits. They are worth doing—even with mediocrity. In time, you will have them developed in stronger patterns and with more regularity. Then, they will become so personalized that you will have a difficult time separating yourself from the habit. We become our habits.

Don't try to develop all eight habits at once. Choose one to work on at a time. Use the discussion questions to stimulate learning with other youth workers. Changing cobwebs into cables takes time and personal discipline. But it's better to choose the cables that build strength into your life than be bound to the cables that imprison you.

If you are lacking motivation, consider the window of time you have to positively impact students. The window is shrinking. We have less and less time to influence youth—we must be more effective. Our kids have less time for youth groups, but when they come, they have higher expectations. They are drop-in/service oriented. They expect quality and service in the limited time they have. They truly are products of the consumer generation.

What is our response to this? Some youth workers lament the days gone by—the "golden days of youth work when we had time with the youth." Others become angry or bitter and accuse kids of being "selfish and materialistic." A healthier response might be to become more effective with the time we *do* have. We need to bend with the trends, but not compromise quality or the message.

Youth workers committed to personal growth are dependent on the Holy Spirit. They know the qualities they seek to develop come out of a vital, dependent relationship with God. They don't seek to manufacture the fruit. The fruit comes as a result of abiding in the Vine. This perspective allows the youth worker to view adversity with new confidence. Instead of running from difficult times or seeing them as sources of doubt, they can become sources for growth. The wise youth worker understands that God uses adversity to develop character that couldn't be developed in times of comfort and ease.

Do not attempt to integrate these habits into your life on your own. You need the support and encouragement of at least one other person. When Jesus sent out his disciples, he sent them out in twos. Who is your "buddy" that can empower you towards excellence?

There is much going on around us which is toxic to our own personal spiritual vitality as well as with our youth. The pace of life causes us to quickly become imbalanced—forgetting the other side of the spectrum. It's easy to ignore our spouse, our children, our physical and spiritual health in the pursuit to perform as youth workers. The competing demands make us vulnerable to destruction from within and without. A burned-out youth worker becomes vulnerable to the world, the flesh, and the devil. As a matter of spiritual warfare, we need to keep ourselves renewed and growing on the cutting edge.

As we usher in a new millennium, youth are looking for a cause to join. They are seeking a purpose they can embrace with their head, heart and hands. We can offer them a model of an explorer on a great adventure. Presenting the cosmic drama of all time—the mystery of the Gospel—which is Christ in us, the hope of glory! This is significant and a cause worth living for. The new millennium lays before us like a blank white board. Youth are searching, "What will be important in the year 2000?" "How should I live my life in this new time?"

As youth workers, we are shapers of the next generation, and we are pioneers of the new millennium. We have within our grasp the potential to build a mighty team of youth, who may impact our culture and the world as no other generation.

It begins with us. It begins from the heart. It begins with habits.

Discussion Questions

1. Which of the "Eight Habits" stands out to you as vital for youth workers?

   ☐ Habit #1: "Effective Youth Workers Are Lifelong Learners"

   ☐ Habit #2: "Effective Youth Workers Are Service-Oriented"

   ☐ Habit #3: "Effective Youth Workers Radiate the Positive Power of the Holy Spirit"

   ☐ Habit #4: "Effective Youth Workers Believe in Others (and Their Growth)"

   ☐ Habit #5: "Effective Youth Workers Lead Balanced Lives"

   ☐ Habit #6: "Effective Youth Workers See Life as an Adventure"

   ☐ Habit #7: "Effective Youth Workers Are Team Players and Synergistic"

   ☐ Habit #8 "Effective Youth Workers Are Committed to Personal Renewal"

2. Why do you think some youth workers *know* what to do, but have a difficult time *implementing* what they know?

3. How can old habits and paradigms keep you from growing fresh and vital habits?

4. In what ways do we as youth workers "dwell on the past" and miss the new things God wants to do? (Isaiah 43:18-19)

5. What do you think about the advice, "If it's worth doing, it's worth doing with mediocrity"?

6. What are some "Baby Steps" you could take to begin applying *one* of these habits to your life?

7. Who will help you with support and encouragement as you "learn to walk" this new habit?

NOTES

1   Denis Waitley, "The Psychology of Winning" in *Ten Qualities of a Total Winner* (tape series) (Niles, IL: Nightingale-Conant Corporation, 1993).

SELF-EVALUATION EXERCISE

Habit #1 *Effective Youth Workers Are Lifelong Learners*

Take the following self-test to see how much of a learner you are. Mark one response.

	Usually	Sometimes	Usually Not
1. I am aware of the trends that effect youth culture.			
2. I see life's experiences as opportunities for learning.			
3. When having a conversation, I listen as much as I talk.			
4. If ministry is finding a need and meeting it, I have a strategy to adjust my ministry as needs in the culture change.			
5. I can think of failures that have been my teachers.			
6. I have others around me to give me input and keep me balanced.			
7. I see the change in our culture as an opportunity to reach people's spiritual needs.			

Scoring: Give yourself a **1** for each "Usually Not", a **2** for each "Sometimes," and a **3** for each "Usually."

  7–11 You've been ditching class.

12–15 Welcome to the elementary school of life.

16–17 Congratulations on graduating into the University of Life.

18–21 You have developed learning as a life skill. Way to go!

SELF-EVALUATION EXERCISE
Habit #2 *Effective Youth Workers Are Service-Oriented*

Use the following questions to evaluate how service-oriented you are.

1. How would you rate your youth work?

Consistent	
Distinctive	
User-Friendly	
Responsive	
Offers Value	

2. Which of the following "Four Ways to Empower through Serving" are strong or weak in your youth ministry?

	Strong	Weak
A. Students discover significance in serving.		
B. Students are empowered toward competence.		
C. Students feel they are a part of a community.		
D. Fun is part of our service projects.		

3. Which of the following assumptions have you had? How have they influenced your view of service and outreach?

A. Teens need to be entertained.

B. Teens don't want to be challenged.

C. Our teens don't have non-Christian friends.

D. Everyone in our group is a Christian.

E. Teens would rather play than serve.

4. To help you draw "outside the line," respond to the following:

What have we done in the past which was successful?

Are we a slave to this?

Has it become a dinosaur?

What might a new approach look like that is totally different in style, but achieve the same purpose?

R E S U L T S

What seems impossible, but if we could do it, would have an incredible impact?

5. Evaluate yourself with the "8 Ways to Serve." Draw a face for your response.

Always   Sometimes   Seldom

A. Return all phone calls within 24 hours.

B. Call students for no reason, just to say "Hi."

C. Inform the parents completely of all details for camps.

D. Take at least one student to lunch each month.

E. Do more listening that talking.

F. Go to student recitals, events, and sporting competitions—especially the ones few attend.

G. Spend time with other youth workers.

H. Drive students places.

SELF-EVALUATION EXERCISE

Habit #3 *Effective Youth Workers*
Radiate the Positive Power of the Holy Spirit

1. What do you think it means to "overflow with hope by the power of the Holy Spirit?" (Romans 15:13)

2. What might you observe in a person under the influence of the Holy Spirit?

3. Which of these qualities is most appealing to you?

4. How would this appealing quality assist you in youth ministry?

5. Study the chart contrasting the Personality Ethic with the Character Ethic on page 58. Which quality under the Character Ethic would you like to see evident in your life?

6. What could you do to develop this character quality, or the desired quality of the Holy Spirit in your life?

7. Describe the steps you can take beginning this week.

SELF-EVALUATION EXERCISE
Habit #4 *Effective Youth Workers Believe in Others (and Their Growth)*

Evaluate your ministry team against the "Eight Goals for an Empowered Team."

	1	2	3	4	5
	Never	Seldom	Sometimes	Often	Always

1. Expect the best from your staff.

2. Know the needs of your students and staff.

3. Establish high standards of excellence.

4. Learn from failure.

5. Promote team spirit (minimize competition).

6. Encourage and model personal renewal.

7. Celebrate achievement and growth.

8. Balance ministry and life (able to say no).

Scoring: Add up the marks for each column and give yourself the value for each response. (1 for Never, 2 for Seldom, etc.)
Empower Team Self-Evaluation Scoring
8–16 Do you have a team?

17–25 You have a start on building your team.

26–34 You obviously are on a growing team.

35–40 Wow! You are on a World-Class Empowered Team!

SELF-EVALUATION EXERCISE
Habit #5 *Effective Youth Workers Lead Balanced Lives*

1. Are you more of a "911 Nancy" (7 day-a-week youth worker) or a "Phil Family Man" (my family always comes first)?

   Explain how each would handle the following scenario:

   > It is 11 P.M. and you are ready for bed. The phone rings and it is Lance, one of the kids in the youth group.

   > "I need to talk with you right now because my parents are being cruel to me. They are totally insane! I hate them!"

   > "What is the problem?"

   > "I don't want to talk about it over the phone, can I come over?"

   How would "911 Nancy" respond?

   How would "Phil Family Man" respond?

2. Make a list of how much time you spend each week in the following competitive time demands.

   <u>Amount of time</u>

   Personal Time

   Ministry Time

   Thought Time

   Activity Time

   Time with Adults

   Time with Students

   Time with Parents

3.   What would the ideal balanced week look like to you?

	Amount of Time	What Would You Do?
Personal Time		
Ministry Time		
Thought Time		
Activity Time		
Time with Adults		
Time with Students		
Time with Parents		

4. Make an ideal weekly schedule that reflects this ideal balance.
   Experiment with it for a week and then revise it.

SUN	MON	TUES	WED	THURS	FRI	SAT

SELF-EVALUATION EXERCISE
Habit #6 *Effective Youth Workers See Life as an Adventure*

1. What makes life adventurous for you?

2. There are three ways to cruise life's journey: as a Traveler, a Tourist, or an Explorer.

> A Traveler just wants to get to his destination. He is focused on getting to the point where he can stop and rest.

> The Tourist enjoys stopping by the side of the road at scenic spots and enjoying the view. He might take a picture, have a picnic, and then get back on the highway.

> The Explorer loves to leave the road most traveled and explore regions unknown. She sees life as an adventure, and is willing to climb a few mountains to capture the view from the summit.

With these three pilgrims in mind, what might each of them do in the following situation?

> *You have been asked to visit one of your sister churches in Guatemala. Your reputation as a youth worker has reached Latin America. "Would you please come to Guatemala and tell us about effective youth work? We will pay for you, your spouse, and one of your key student leaders to come and help us."*

> *You consider the two-week mission. "All expenses paid and a unique opportunity for me, my spouse, and one lucky kid."*

The **Traveler** would:

The **Tourist** would:

The **Explorer** would:

SELF-EVALUATION EXERCISE

Habit #7 *Effective Youth Workers Are Team Players and Synergistic*

1. A Producer is one who develops new ideas and products. A Manager coordinates the work and the workers. The Leader sets the vision and direction for the team. Which of these roles best describes your role in youth work? Why?

2. Effective teams have discovered how to affirm each member's uniqueness. They make it their goal to make each person's strength more productive, and each weakness more irrelevant. These efforts lead to synergy—the state in which the whole is more than the sum of the parts. Synergistic youth work seeks to affirm the value and contribution of each youth worker. How does this style of ministry compare to the scriptural accounts in 1 Corinthians 12 and Ephesians 4:1-16?

3. To build your team, you may need a paradigm shift. Review the material in the Team Builder Paradigm Shift on pages 111 and 113.

   How are you doing on the following paradigm shifts?

   From: PROGRAM to PEOPLE
   PRODUCTION to PRINCIPLES
   PAST to FUTURE
   OBSTACLES to OPPORTUNITIES
   FEAR OF CRITICISM to CULTURAL RELEVANCE

4. Take another look at the 20 qualities of The Effective Team Leader on page 119.

   Which of these qualities are evident in your team now?

   Which of these qualities are evident some of the time, or with some of the team members?

   Which of these qualities are seldom seen on your team?

   Pick two of the qualities you would like to see more of on your youth ministry team.
   1.
   2.

5. What could you do to help these two qualities of The Effective Team Leader, in yourself and others on your team?

SELF-EVALUATION EXERCISE
Habit #8 *Effective Youth Workers Are Committed to Personal Renewal*

Burnout Potential Quiz
Respond by recording a number that best represents the frequency.

10 9 8 7 6 5 4 3 2 1
Always-Frequent-Sometimes-Seldom-Never

1. I find myself skipping meals.

2. I talk on the phone when I
   should be sleeping.

3. Phone calls interrupt dinner.

4. I'm out five or more nights
   a week.

5. I have exercise less than
   twice a week.

6. I skip my times alone with
   God.

7. My time for myself is overlooked.

8. I have friends to support me.

9. I have a regular hobby that
   I enjoy.

10. I take a full day off weekly.

11. I read books for inspiration.

12. I limit the amount of TV I
    watch.

13. I journal or take time just
    to think.

14. My study time is separate
    from my personal spiritual
    renewal.

Scoring:

1. Add up the values from questions #1-7. Enter the total here: _____

> 70-60   Burnout is inevitable.
>
> 59-49   Burnout is likely.
>
> 48-30   Fifty percent chance of burnout.
>
> 29-18   You are good at personal renewal.
>
> 17-7   You are totally charged. Burnout is highly unlikely.

2. Add up the values from questions #8-14. Enter the total here: _____

> 70-60   You have mastered self-renewal
>
> 59-49   You show skill in personal renewal
>
> 48-30   Your personal renewal skills need strengthening
>
> 29-18   Have you ever considered personal renewal?
>
> 17-7   You're speeding toward destruction on the Burnout Express.

3. As a result of this information about myself, I plan to:
   (Describe a short strategy for change, if you need to.)

My Favorite Books for Youth Workers

Back to the Heart of Youthwork, Dewey Bertolini, Victor Books, Wheaton, IL, 1989.

> Dewey raises the standard of integrity as a hallmark for the character of the youth worker.

Boundaries, Drs. Henry Cloud and John Townsend, Zondervan Publishing House, Grand Rapids, MI, 1992.

> Many youth workers find themselves in burnout. This excellent resource helps the reader learn to say "no."

Bringing Out the Best in People, Alan Loy McGinnis, Augsburg Publishing House, Minneapolis, MN, 1985.

> A positive, practical, and motivational book. A necessary resource for all leaders and managers.

Children without Childhood, Marie Winn, Pantheon Books, NY, 1993.

> A penetrating look at our culture and how we rush children through childhood.

A Church for the 21st Century, Leith Anderson, Bethany House Publishers, Minneapolis, MN, 1992.

> A helpful prescription of the effective church and youth group in the new millennium.

The Coming Revolution in Youth Ministry, Mark Senter III, Victor Books, Wheaton, IL, 1992.

> One of the most thought-provoking books on youth ministry I've read in years. It helps us understand our past, and hopefully, our future.

Counseling Teenagers, Dr. G. Keith Olson, Thom Schultz Publications, Inc., Loveland, CO, 1984.

> A useful tool for ideas on counseling adolescents. Appropriate for volunteers and full-time youth workers.

Create in Me a Youth Ministry, Ridge Burns and Pam Campbell, Victor Books, Wheaton, IL, 1986, 1994.

> Practical, basic, and from the heart. In other words, "Classic Ridge Burns." I liked the discussion on burnout and the Small Church Spotlight. A good resource for volunteer youth workers.

Enjoy Your Middle Schooler, Wayne Rice, Zondervan Publishing House, Grand Rapids, MI, 1994.

> Six easy-to-read chapters on "The Wonder Years." Parents and youth workers discover key insights on the physical, emotional, social, intellectual, and spiritual development of young adolescents.

Feeding Your Forgotten Soul, Paul Borthwick, Zondervan Publishing House, Grand Rapids, MI, 1990.

> Youth work demands spiritual energy. Paul Borthwick sensitively deals with the drain of our souls and how we can stop it.

Growing Up Christian, Jim Marian, Victor Books, Wheaton, IL, 1992.

> "Teens that have grown up in the church *are* different," says Jim Marian. In this helpful book you'll discover how they are different and what you can do to help them grow and develop their faith.

Growing Up in America, Anthony Campolo, Zondervan Publishing House, Grand Rapids, MI, 1989.

> The subtitle is "A Sociology of Youth Ministry" but don't let that scare you. This book will help you understand the world of the American teenager. It introduces the reader to some of the barriers we face in our culture, as we seek to reach youth.

Help! I'm a Volunteer Youth Worker, Doug Fields, Zondervan Publishing House, Grand Rapids, MI, 1992.

> We give this book to each of our volunteers as a basic introduction to youth ministry. It offers fifty bite-size suggestions that are user-friendly and do-able.

Helping the Struggling Adolescent, Les Parrott III, Zondervan Publishing House, Grand Rapids, MI, 1993.

> Get help for thirty problems that you are bound to encounter as a youth worker. Easy to use and comprehensive.

"Hi, I'm Bob and I'm the Parent of a Teenager"–A Guide to Beginning and Leading a Support Group for Parents of Teens, Tim Smith, Regal Books, Ventura, CA, 1991.

> A guide to beginning and leading a support group for parents of teens. It can also be used as a class for parents. Topics include: building self-esteem, values, communication, and resolving conflict.

High School Ministry, Mike Yaconelli and Jim Burns, Zondervan Publishing House, Grand Rapids, MI, 1986.

> An insightful look at high school culture and how to impact it. Specific strategies and activities are included.

How to Work with Rude, Obnoxious and Apathetic Kids, Les Christie, Victor Books, Wheaton, IL, 1994.

> Distracting, undisciplined teens can ruin a youth group. Learn how these problems can be opportunities to positively influence the rowdy kids in your group.

In Search of Excellence, Thomas Peters and Robert H. Waterman Jr., Warner Books, NY, 1982.

> The classic business book on excellence. I use it for discussions with our team on how we can develop excellence in youth work.

Junior High Ministry, Wayne Rice, Zondervan Publishing House, Grand Rapids, MI, 1987.

> The best book on the junior high ministry that I am aware of. Wayne Rice really understands the changes and challenges of early adolescence. Also combined are fifty pages of ideas, making this book a very practical program resource.

Keeping Your Teen in Touch with God, Dr. Robert Laurent, David C. Cook Publishing Co., Elgin, IL, 1988.

> Why some church kids lose their interest in spiritual matters, and what you can do to help.

My Utmost for His Highest, Oswald Chambers, Discovery House Publishers, Grand Rapids, MI, 1992.

> A classic, penetrating devotional.

No Youth Worker Is an Island, Ridge Burns and Pam Campbell, Victor Books, Wheaton, IL, 1992.

> Simple, easy-to-read advice on ten key issues of youth work. The Small Church Spotlight appeals to volunteers.

Organizing Your Youth Ministry, Paul Borthwick, Zondervan Publishing House, Grand Rapids, MI, 1988.

> Organization is often the downfall of youth workers. This book provides realistic and helpful steps to becoming more organized.

Principle-Centered Leadership, Stephen R. Covey, Fireside Books, Simon Schuster Inc., NY, 1992.

> Picking up where *Seven Habits* leaves off; Covey develops the theme of character and leadership.

The Pro Teen Parent, Daniel Hahn, Questar Publishers Inc., Sisters, OR, 1992.

> Ten practical and tested ways for parents and youth workers to encourage spiritual growth in teens.

Radical Respect (previously titled *Handling Your Hormones*, 1986), Jim Burns, Harvest House Publishers, Eugene, OR, 1992.

> My favorite resource for talking to teens about love and sexuality. A great resource for a course on sexuality.

Reaching Out to Troubled Youth, Dwight Spotts and David Veerman, Victor Books, Wheaton, IL, 1987, 1994.

> This book helps the youth worker handle problem situations and prepares him/her to positively influence teens at risk.

The Seven Habits of Highly Effective People, Stephen Covey, Fireside Books, Simon & Schuster Inc., NY, 1989.

> Youth work is not simply a set of skills, but a matter of habits; of passion, principles and patterns of behavior. Covey introduces seven habits that have relevant application to youth ministry.

Surviving Adolescence or Growing Up Oughta Be Easier than This!, Jim Burns, Word Publishing, Dallas, TX, 1990.

> This book will help the youth worker influence teens to make positive choices and prevent them from making negative ones. Jim Burns challenges teens not to settle for second best. The study guide makes this a useful resource for group study and discussion.

User-Friendly Churches, George Barna, Regal Books, Ventura, CA, 1991.

> Evaluate how friendly your youth group is by learning from Barna about what makes groups/churches "friendly."

The Youth Builder, Jim Burns, Harvest House Publishers, Eugene, OR, 1988.

> The primer for youth ministry. This book lays a solid foundation, and then builds a practical infrastructure for effective ministry.

The Youth Minister's Survival Guide, Len Kageler, Zondervan Publishing House, Grand Rapids, MI, 1992.

> I have met creative, talented, and popular youth workers who disqualify themselves because of the basics. Kageler reviews the basic rules of effective youth work—rules, that if followed, will help youth workers avoid disqualification.

Tim Smith is available for consulting and speaking to:

- Youth workers
- Teens
- Parents
- Business Leaders/Managers
- Churches and Conferences

For a detailed brochure of seminars, or to inquire about Tim speaking at your event, write:

WORDSMITH

Tim Smith

P.O. Box 7736

Thousand Oaks, CA 91359-7736